Joshua

Heaven's Mighty Warrior

Sheryl Pellatiro

For more information on other resources available, and ministry opportunities, please visit our website at:

www.solidtruthministries.com

Copyright © 2017 Sheryl Pellatiro. All rights reserved. No part of this publication may be reproduced or transmitted in any form or by any means, electronic or mechanical, including photocopying, recording, or any information storage and retrieval system, without permission in writing from the author.

Unless otherwise noted, all Scripture quotations are from the Holy Bible; New International Version®, Copyright© 1973, 1978, 1984 by International Bible Society.

The "NIV" and "New International Version" trademarks are registered in the United States Patent and Trademark office by International Bible Society.

ISBN – 1978413459
ISBN – 978-1978413450

Contact Information:

Solid Truth Ministries, Inc.
www.solidtruthministries.com
www.sherylpellatiro.com
sheryl@solidtruthministries.com

No one will be able to stand up against you all the days of your life. As I was with Moses, so I will be with you; I will never leave you nor forsake you.

Joshua 1:5

Dedication:

To Joshua!

Your legacy lives on in the hearts

of everyone who dares to study the

book named after you. You were truly

one of Heaven's mightiest warriors! In addition

to your great leadership qualities, your love

and devotion to your God has inspired us

in our quest to move forward with God.

Table of Contents

Introduction..7

Week 1:   **A Warrior in Training**..............................9
                     Day 1 – God's Plan in Motion
                     Day 2 – Background Check
                     Day 3 – First Battle
                     Day 4 – Joshua the Servant
                     Day 5 – The Faith of a Warrior

Week 2:   **A Warrior Set Apart**..............................27
                     Day 1 – The Commissioning
                     Day 2 – Taking the Reins
                     Day 3 – Great Instruction
                     Day 4 – Spiritual Chain of Command
                     Day 5 – An Unlikely Heroine

Week 3:   **Moving Forward**..................................45
                     Day 1 – Insurmountable Impasse
                     Day 2 – Ark of the Covenant
                     Day 3 – One Important Detail
                     Day 4 – Crossing the Jordan
                     Day 5 – Twelve Stones

Week 4:   **Conquering Jericho**.............................62
                     Day 1 – Circumcision and Celebration
                     Day 2 – The Commander's Appearance
                     Day 3 – God's Battle Plan
                     Day 4 – Redemptive Purposes
                     Day 5 – A Fatal Mistake

Week 5:   **Marching Fearlessly**............................82
                     Day 1 – Brilliant Strategy
                     Day 2 – Deceived and Defrauded
                     Day 3 – Audacious Faith
                     Day 4 – Conquering the land
                     Day 5 – Fighting Offensively

Week 6:   Settling the Land..101
        Day 1 – Never Too Old
        Day 2 – Painful Misunderstanding
        Day 3 – Farewell Address
        Day 4 – Covenant Renewal
        Day 5 – Finishing Strong

About the Author..117

Other Bible Studies..118

Mission Statement..119

Introduction

Not long ago, Anne Graham Lotz said: *"I can feel the encroaching darkness of evil that is like a heavy moral and spiritual fog. The enemy is advancing and permeating our nation at every level."* She goes on to say that *"God commands us to arise, let our Light shine, so the distinctive glory of our Lord will be obvious to all."*[1]

I couldn't agree more. Satan knows his time is of the essence, so he is on a destructive warpath and is determined to bring the Church down one pillar at a time. The war is escalating and will continue to do so until Jesus comes back for His people.

So here's a reality we need to understand: the United States seems to be under attack. Persecution for Christians is becoming more prevalent. Over the last several decades things have worsened. We have certainly seen a rise in anti-Christian hostility. People with no regard for God have been elected to lead. God is being pushed out. And our freedoms are slowly being taken away.

Friend, this is called war. Spiritual war. There are two sides to this war: the good side led by the Commander of the Armies, God Himself... and the evil side led by the master deceiver and the greatest enemy of God, Satan. It's a fierce war! Believers stand on the battleground, vulnerable and under attack. Satan is smart and crafty. He knows the best way to hurt God and destroy what He has built up is to pursue God's people. And he pursues us with a vengeance. It is his goal to bring you and me down.

Whether we like it or not, we are called to the front lines. We're drafted. A sobering reality is that most Christians are unprepared for this war. We have no clue how to fight. No earthly training could prepare us for this war, because *this* war cannot be conquered with human weapons. I believe God is looking for great warriors who will fight.

This brings us to our study on Joshua. Truly one of the greatest heroes of the Old Testament, Joshua led the Israelites into the Promised Land. Joshua served as a military leader, a political leader, and a spiritual leader. He proved to be battlefield genius, particularly in the areas of careful planning, strategy, and execution. Joshua challenged his people by both word and example.

Now, in relation to the war we currently face—a war that is heating up—there may not be a better person, or book of the Bible, to help us become mighty warriors for God's Army. Warriors with whom God will be pleased! The Nation of Israel was blessed under Joshua's leadership. We read at the end of Joshua:

"The people of Israel served the LORD throughout the lifetime of Joshua and of the elders who outlived him - those who had personally experienced all that the LORD had done for Israel." -- Joshua 24:31

I hope you're ready for some serious training. Everything we study in the Old Testament, we will apply to our current life here in the 21st century as the Bible is timeless. Something tells me that we will discover unforeseen things we never imagined important for *this* military training. We're in this together, both learning and striving toward a holiness that honors God and leads to success in this battle.

In the end, I believe that you and I will be counted among God's greatest warriors. Don't back down! Don't get discouraged! And keep your eyes focused on the victory that will be celebrated at the end of the war.

1.https://www.facebook.com/AnneGrahamLotz/posts/10154132330522476?comment_id=10154132384022476&comment_tracking=%7B%22tn%22%3A%22R%22%7D

Week 1
A Warrior in Training

Day 1
God's Plan in Motion
Day 2
Background Check
Day 3
First Battle
Day 4
Joshua the Servant
Day 5
The Faith of a Warrior

    I love starting new Bible studies. I love the challenge. I love the research. I love the findings. And I love how it stretches me spiritually. I never know how the Holy Spirit will use it in my life or others' lives. My goal with each study is to bring life to the Word of God and to show how biblical principles can be applied to our lives. I know that I need the study of God's Word as much as you do.

    As I look toward our study in Joshua, let me point out some interesting things we will find. Joshua was born into slavery, but rose to become a great military leader and commander. He was a soldier, a servant, a spy, and a successor. The secret to Joshua's success was his faith in the Word of God (**Joshua 1:7-9**), its commandments, and its promises. Joshua obeyed God while leading the people into their new awaited land.

    The book of Joshua records battles, defeats, sins, and failures. It also illustrates how believers today can bid good-bye to the old life and enter into a rich inheritance in Jesus Christ. It explains how we can face off – and defeat – our enemies, and how to claim for ourselves all that we have in Jesus Christ. We will see how Joshua is really a foretelling of what is ours in Christ. Like the land of plenty He promised the Israelites, God has promised us a fruitful life we can enjoy as well.

    With that said, I can't wait to see the fruit of this work. I can't wait to see how our study on Joshua will impact you, God's faithful servants. In addition to gleaning from the *book* of Joshua, we will also look at Joshua the *man*. Why did God choose him? What made Joshua such a mighty warrior and leader? I'm praying that God will open our eyes and show us great and awe-inspiring things. I'm praying that this study will be the tool God will use to launch us into a new adventure with Him and prepare us for what's in store.

Day 1
God's Plan in Motion

Look up **Exodus 3:8**. Please fill in the blanks:

So I have come down to _____ them from the hand of the Egyptians and to bring them up out of that land into a _____ and _____ land, a land _____ with _____ and _____...

Before we delve into Joshua, it's important we gain some background information first. This will set the stage for our study. The book of Genesis records the beginning of God's chosen people. It begins with the creation and concludes with Jacob and his family fleeing to Egypt because their homeland was suffering from a severe famine. God's people then became enslaved in Egypt for four hundred years.

Now, summarize the events of Israel's early years in Egypt based on **Exodus 1:1-7**.

The descendants of Jacob numbered seventy in all. We read that they were fruitful and multiplied and the land was filled with them (**Exodus 1:7**). This was truly the beginning of God's promise to Abraham: **"I will confirm my covenant between me and you and will greatly increase your numbers" (Genesis 17:2).**

Before they arrived in Egypt, the chosen people of God had a limited understanding of their God. The greater knowledge would come later, when they were dwelling in the desert. Still, four hundred years is a long time for a nation to become immersed in another culture. I wonder if, over time, they strayed from their own religious practices and fell into the Egyptian culture and worshiped the Egyptian gods.

Write down what you think it was like for the Israelites living in Egypt. What do you envision?

While the people grew and multiplied in Egypt, they were also slaves for four centuries. As time went on, a new king in Egypt came to power—a king who did not know Joseph, and one who seemed to have little concern for God's people. Eventually, he made life unbearable for the Israelites (**Exodus 1:8-10**).

According to **Exodus 1:10**, why did the Egyptians make life difficult for God's people?

What kinds of difficulties did God's people face (**Exodus 1:11-14**)?

What else do you learn about their life in Egypt from **Exodus 1:15-21**?

Without a doubt, the Israelites were stuck. They were miserable. And the king of Egypt didn't care about them. They struggled to survive under such harsh conditions. A perfect picture of slavery.

Here's the thing: slavery wasn't just prominent in the past – it still exists in the church today. In fact, a high percentage of believers are chained up and living in captivity. No one is happy living this way. Slavery is anything that has *master* over you.

What truth is found in **Galatians 5:1**?

What title does Paul give himself in **Philippians 1:1**?

The insight I gather from the previous verses is that I do *not* have to live as a slave because Jesus *died* for my freedom. But being a slave—or a servant—to Jesus is different from being a slave to the flesh, sin, or Satan. Allowing sin, bondage, my past, fear, pride, or human nature to rule over me prevents me from enjoying the full life I was meant to have in Christ. Jesus said, **"I have come that they may have life, and have it to the full" (John 10:10)**. So letting Jesus be master over me puts me on a pathway to victory.

Which master will you choose? What is your plan of action?

In relation to the nation of Israel, God would never let His people live in slavery forever. He had a plan! A glorious plan! After four hundred years in Egypt, the nation numbered over two million people.

How did the Israelites react to the harsh labor imposed on them (**Exodus 2:23**)?

How did God respond to the people (**Exodus 2:24-25**)?

Read **Exodus 3:1-10**.

Moses was an unlikely candidate for this massive work. He was raised in the Egyptian palace of Pharaoh, but fled Egypt after he killed a man and Pharaoh sought to kill him (**Exodus 2:11-15**). For the next forty years, Moses lived in Midian, a little town far from Egypt. We don't learn much about his life during that time, but we do know that he tended sheep. Something tells me that life in Midian had become comfortable. When we have not-so-good memories of a place and we've moved on, we usually don't have a desire to revisit that place. I imagine Moses felt the same way about Egypt. But, God had other plans.

Answer the following questions based on **Exodus 3:7-8**:

What was God's plan?

What was God's promise?

Write out the description of the land God was going to give to His people.

God described a land that was rich, fertile and desirable—a land He would give to His people for their enjoyment. Imagine the gleam in their eyes when they heard this. God was not only going to deliver them from the harsh conditions of Egypt, but He was promising them a beautiful land. A land they could call their own. A land they could put down roots. Such hope in their otherwise gloomy world.

The promise and hope God gave to the Israelites is a picture of what He's promised us. Give a brief description of your future home based on **Revelation 21:1-4**.

Not long ago, my friend and her family went on a mission trip to Haiti. As my friend ministered among the people, she was drawn to this one particular lady—a lady who lived in squalor conditions, but radiated joy. When my friend asked this lady what gave her such joy, she simply stated that she keeps her eyes focused on the life awaiting her—her new home in heaven.

The people of God struggled to survive in Egypt. The conditions were horrible. So, I'm guessing that once they heard the good news Moses brought, they kept their eyes focused on the Promised Land. We may live in America, the land of plenty, but we also live in a distorted world—a world where sin is rampant. In this place we face hurt, pain, temptation, and disease every day. But the good news is that God has promised to take us away from all this one day—to a true promised land.

The other day God spoke to me about my future home:

"Remember child that one day there will be no more pain or sorrow. There will be no more dark nights or dreary days. One day you'll have a brand new body perfectly suited for heaven. And in this place, you'll be reunited with your loved ones - they are waiting for your arrival - and you will meet many new ones. Your life in heaven will far exceed anything you've ever experienced on earth. It will all be yours one day and the rewards for a faithful life will be poured out."

Aren't you excited?

So let me ask you: Will you do as so many others have done? Will you fix your eyes on what's ahead, what God has promised? How will you do this?

Stay with me as we continue to move closer to God fulfilling one of the greatest promises ever recorded in Scripture.

Write down what you gained from today's lesson. What did God speak to you about?

Day 2
Background Check

When I applied to become a school bus driver, a background check was conducted to make sure I didn't have anything from my past that could affect my performance driving students. This is common practice in the day in which we live. Many companies run a background check on potential employees. It's a safeguard for them.

Of course, God doesn't have to do that since He knows you and I so well, but our background can play an important role in the job He chooses for us. However, His credentials are usually in stark contrast to what we think they should be. In fact, He often chooses unlikely candidates. Moses certainly fits into this category.

In addition to Moses, here are a few other biblical characters who appear to be unlikely candidates. Take note of their background and their future work.

Who?	Background	Future Work
David	Shepherd, targeted by Saul, lived in the caves	King of Israel
Jonah	Ran away from God	Prophet
Gideon	Harvester of wheat, from weak clan	Rescuer of Israel from Midianites
Peter	Fisherman	Apostle, pillar of early church, writer
Matthew	Tax collector	Disciple
Mary Magdalene	Demon possessed	Jesus' follower and helper
Samaritan Woman	Adulterer, outcast	Influenced her community for Christ
Paul	Persecutor of Christians, murderer	Evangelist, leader of early church, wrote majority of New Testament
Priscilla and Aquila	Tentmakers	Helpers of the apostle Paul

What is the apostle Paul's testimony, according to **1 Corinthians 2:1-5**?

Why does God choose the unlikely candidate for His work **(1 Corinthians 2:5)**?

If you are weak, then you are perfect to carry out a kingdom work. If you tremble at the task God has put before you but still move forward with it, then you demonstrate God's power more. If you think you're not qualified, well, you really aren't. Then again, this is exactly the ones He chooses. He often puts before us a work we feel unqualified to handle. Why? *Because our weakness demonstrates the Spirit's power!* Some of the most influential people in the Christian arena today come with sordid backgrounds. Their past should have driven them into a life of turmoil. And sometimes they started out that way. But then God got ahold of them and Jesus healed their brokenness. Eventually, they became great ambassadors for God's kingdom.

Throughout Scripture, we find unlikely candidates. The same is true for Joshua. Let's look at a couple things in his background:

Joshua was born into slavery!

Joshua was born in Egypt at the time when the Israelites were being mistreated. He was a young man when his people exited Egypt with Moses as their commander. He spent quite a long time enmeshed in a place where harsh treatment was a way of life.

What do you think life was like for Joshua in Egypt?

When you think of slavery, what comes to your mind?

Of course, we've read books and watched shows on early slavery. Therefore, we have images in our mind of what slaves endured at the hands of their owners. Some were treated as part of the family, but others were handled like a piece of trash—as mere property. Many of them, I'm sure, lacked confidence. They may have been filled with bitterness as well. They loathed their owners, but were not in a position to do anything about it. So day after day, week after week, year after year, they simply went about their chores, with little passion trying not to displease their masters.

We don't have to guess what life was like for Joshua and his people in Egypt. The Bible tells us that **"they put slave masters over them to oppress them with forced labor… and worked them ruthlessly… and made their lives bitter with hard labor" (Exodus 1:11, 13-14).** For many years, this is what Joshua witnessed and what he experienced firsthand. He saw hatred in the eyes of his people. They were miserable. And where misery pervades, dissension, discord, and chaos usually rear their ugly heads.

Have you witnessed this kind of misery? What was the atmosphere like?

During those long dark days in Egypt, there may have been some that tried to keep the morale up – those who chose to be positive influencers. But I imagine that around many dinner tables, moms and dads, sisters and brothers, found negativity the norm.

I was just telling my kids how things have changed in our country since I was growing up. I believe it's entirely possible that we may become slaves, like Joshua was in Egypt, in our country one day, ruled by people who have no regard for God.

Read Jesus' words in **Matthew 5:10-12** and answer the following questions.

How should we respond to harsh treatment?

What happens to those who are persecuted?

Now let's cover the second piece to Joshua's background…

Joshua was a servant!

What do you learn about Joshua from the following verses?

Exodus 24:13:

Exodus 33:11:

Numbers 11:28:

We will come back to these verses for different purposes as we move along in our study, but I'm guessing you wrote down that Joshua was Moses' aide since he was young.

The Hebrew word for "aide" is *sarat* and means "to minister, serve or attend."

Now, here's the thing: the position that Joshua held as Moses' servant may or may not have been the perfect credentials for successor. Let's talk about why this job may have made Joshua an unlikely candidate for great kingdom work and leadership.

Joshua was always in the background. Behind the scenes, so to speak. Moses was the one who talked to the people, led them through the wilderness, and received the commandments. He was in charge. Moses wore very big shoes and the people respected him.

People with a servant heart are often overlooked in the bigger picture. We often notice the people on stage, the ones who are vocal, and the gregarious leaders. But the servants usually take a back seat and that's just fine with them. Most servants I know do not want to be noticed. Perhaps this fits Joshua as well. He loved being with Moses. He loved serving him. Moses was the one who heard from God. Joshua was called to be his helper.

When you look at it like this, I think this surely makes Joshua an unlikely candidate.

What do you think Joshua's day was like – as Moses aide? What do you think he learned from his teacher?

What does Jesus teach His disciples about being a servant in **John 13:12-17**?

What does Jesus' teaching mean to you? How will you apply it to your life?

Here's one last question: Based on what you learned about Joshua, and what Jesus said, why do you think God may have chosen Joshua for such a commanding job?

Day 3
First Battle

Before we move forward into the first battle, there is one more detail we need to learn about Joshua. An important one!

What do you learn about Joshua's name in **Numbers 13:16**?

The Hebrew name *Joshua* means, "Yahweh is salvation, deliverer." Here's the interesting thing: The name *Jesus* is the Greek derivative of Joshua. Many scholars believe that Joshua was a type of Christ. In addition to his name, look at the following chart for a few comparisons:

Joshua	Jesus
Servant of Moses	Took on the nature of a servant (Philippians 2:6-7).
Commander of Israel	Commander of heaven and earth (Matthew 28:18).
Led Israel into their Promised Land	Will lead His people to their awaited Promised Land (John 14:2-3).
Mighty conqueror	The mighty conqueror over sin and death (1 Corinthians 15:57).
A faithful leader	Our merciful and faithful high priest (Hebrews 2:17).

Jesus is the central theme of the entire Bible. The *Old Testament* points toward the Messiah who would come to deliver His people from sin and death; the *Gospels* (Matthew – John) show the fulfillment of the Messiah; *Acts* follows the expansion of the early church with Jesus as the foundation; the *Epistles* (Romans–3 John) look back at Jesus, the cross and His resurrection; and *Revelation* looks toward the future prophesies about Jesus.

Obviously we can see the picture of Christ in Joshua.

How does this truth open up Scripture to you?

Let's now move into the first battle. This is the first time in Scripture we encounter Joshua. And it's also the first battle recorded. Read **Exodus 17:8-16** and summarize briefly.

I have read this story countless times and each time, my heart skips a couple beats. Today's story isn't just about an Old Testament battle between Israel and her enemies, but it's also about the battle each of us face on a daily basis: the battle of our flesh against God's greatest enemy. It's important to remember that this war is taking place in the spiritual realm, and if we choose to fight like Israel's leaders, we *can* emerge a victor. Let's take a deeper look.

Who was chosen to be the commander on the battlefield (**verse 9**)?

According to **Exodus 17:9-10**, where was Moses, Aaron and Hur positioned?

Write down what happened on the top of the hill (**Exodus 17:11-13**).

What did Joshua fight with, according to **Exodus 17:13**?

Did the Israelites see victory this day? Explain.

There are two important things happening in this battle we need to address. One is on top of the hill, and the other is down in the valley. Let's look at both of them.

On top of the hill!

The raising of hands represents the *power of prayer*!

When were the Israelites winning the war (**Exodus 17:11**)?

Did Moses handle this task alone (**Exodus 17:12**)? Write down the details.

While Joshua and his army battled it out in the valley, Moses stood on top of the mountain holding up the staff of God. The *staff of God* represents the almighty power of God.[3] Did you notice that Moses wasn't alone? Aaron and Hur stood on either side of him, and when his arms grew tired, they held up his hands until sunset. Friends, there is not a more glorious picture of prayer warriors than this one right here.

Read **2 Corinthians 1:8-11**. Write down what Paul was going through and how believers helped him.

The work God has called me to do is challenging and surely outside my comfort zone. And I could never do it without prayer warriors. Whenever I'm called upon to speak in public, I think of this story in Exodus and this passage in 2 Corinthians. Then I gather my prayer warriors. I'm not afraid to ask for prayer. You shouldn't be either. We are supposed to come alongside one another and hold each other up in prayer.

If you're facing a difficulty, fearful of an outcome, worried for a loved one, struggling in some area, or overcome by unforeseen circumstances, ask for prayer. If the work God has put before you seems too daunting and you feel inadequate, ask for prayer. If the enemy is in hot pursuit of your mind and your flesh, make sure to ask for prayer. Let God's faithful ones stand on each side of you and hold your hands up.

By allowing prayer warriors to come to your aid, you are letting God fight for you. And then those warriors become His instruments for a glorious outcome. Do I hear an *Amen*?

In the valley!

The sword represents the *power of God's Word*.

What is the Word of God called in **Ephesians 6:17**?

What does a sword represent to you?

If you wrote that a sword represents a "weapon" or a "tool" to use in combat, then we are on the same page. Only this weapon is not for an earthly fight. On the contrary!

What does the apostle Paul say about this weapon in **2 Corinthians 10:4**?

That's right! The Word of God gives us the upper hand against our enemy. But we must use it in that manner. If you are facing off with the enemy right now—maybe in your thoughts, your flesh, or your spirit—then you can hold God's Word out and command your enemy to flee. Satan cannot stand up against God's holy Word. He will run every time. With these divine weapons at our disposal, I guess it's safe to say that the only power Satan has over us is the power we let him have.

I utilize this powerful weapon almost daily. The devil is often hot on my tail and he may be hot on yours, too. He knows what buttons to push—the ones that might cause you to sin or to turn from God. And trust me; he has plenty of tricks up his sleeve. But the Word of God will ward him off every time. Let's use it, my friends. Quote it out loud, while stomping on the ground commanding his removal. God's Word is God's Word! He spoke it into existence. It's powerful and it's ours to use.

How will you fight your battles today?

Now, let's go back to our story at hand in Exodus. In the end, who won the war—God or the Israelites? Explain.

What happened after the war (**Exodus 17:14-16**)?

God wanted them to remember *how* the war was won. And then it ends on a glorious note with Moses giving the glory to God. What a beautiful picture for us to breathe in.

It's important to note that both aspects—the raising up of the hands on the hill, and the drawn sword in the valley—were both equally important in winning this battle. Prayer and the Word of God always work best together. We can look at Moses holding up the staff of God as a picture of us letting God do the fighting. By utilizing prayer and God's Word, we are surely passing the baton on to God. And it's always His privilege to fight for us.

So my friends gather your prayer warriors and grab your Bible as you face off with your greatest enemy. And then, when it's said and done, don't forget to give God the glory. He deserves our praise, honor and worship.

What did God speak to you about today? Write down your thoughts.

Day 4
Joshua the Servant

We briefly looked at this topic earlier in our study, but today I want to investigate servanthood a little deeper since it's an important subject in Scripture. Let me begin by saying that the one being served is blessed, but the one serving is blessed the most. If you've been on both sides, you may be nodding your head in agreement. You know!

Take in mind that what we're learning about Joshua is preparing him for the biggest challenge and work of his life.

What early position did Joshua hold, according to **Numbers 11:28**?

Now let's look at the context. Read **Numbers 11:26-29**. What do you learn about Moses and Joshua?

Joshua was Moses' aide from youth. We don't know how old he was at this recording, but he was still serving Moses. As the leader of the Israelites, I imagine Moses' plate was pretty full. It must have been wonderful relying on Joshua to help. Perhaps Joshua got things ready for Moses when he arrived at the tabernacle for morning sacrifices. Maybe he brought food, handled the administrative stuff, and kept the place neat and orderly. Joshua took the load off Moses and did whatever needed to be done. Something tells me that Joshua also did it with joy.

Joshua looked up to Moses as his esteemed leader and mentor. But remember, Joshua was still young and had a lot to learn. I've often said that you need to be a follower before becoming a leader. Everyone needs to learn from others who are more mature. Moses had been through a lot and had matured in his faith since the days tending sheep. And the situation before us today is a perfect example of someone younger learning from someone older and wiser.

What does **Numbers 12:3** tell you about Moses?

Compare what you just learned about Moses with **Numbers 11:29**.

In this case, I think Joshua was just looking out after his mentor. Moses was the one who had a front row seat to God's throne room, and he was the one who usually spoke on behalf of God. I think Joshua felt it was his responsibility to look out after Moses. So when two men rose up and began to prophesy, he thought they should be stopped. He certainly did not understand the all-encompassing power of God and His Spirit. And he didn't see that the Spirit really did rest on them. But Moses, who was much more in tune with God, did.

Another thing we cannot overlook is that Moses shows great security in his role as leader. Leaders who are secure in the position God has placed them never get jealous of others using their gifts. Moses said to Joshua, **"I wish that all the LORD'S people were prophets and that the LORD would put his Spirit on them" (Numbers 11:29).**

Joshua probably did not know that by serving Moses, God was preparing him for his future work. And he was learning from the humblest of all men on the earth. When I joined the women's team at my church recently, I was asked if I wanted to mentor someone younger in the faith or to be mentored by someone. Since I do a lot of mentoring, I chose to learn from someone older and wiser. So I was paired up with the wife of our former pastor. She's 90 years old.

I had never met Libby before, but when we sat down for lunch, I was incredibly moved by her story. She is the author of many books, a former pilot, and still teaches a woman's study at 6:30 in the morning. She is one of the most humble women I have ever met. And she certainly demonstrates a servant heart. I have had many mentors in my life. And I've learned valuable lessons from each of them as I continue to follow God and lead His people into the Word of God. Oh how thankful I am that I, like Joshua, could sit under such great servants.

Do you have a mentor you look up to? A humble servant? If not, make sure to find one.

Later in life, Joshua probably looked back and thanked God for the lessons he learned from his humble teacher, Moses.

I don't think there is another role that warms God's heart as much as servanthood. In fact, the Bible has a lot to say about it. Let's take a look…

Write out what you learn about serving others.

Matthew 20:20-28:

Galatians 5:13:

Ephesians 6:7-8:

1 Peter 5:2-3:

According to **1 Peter 5:4**, how will God reward servants?

There is so much more we could cover on servanthood, but we just don't have the time. I will say though that the Bible teaches us that in God's kingdom, servanthood ranks higher than anything else. Something tells me that the places of honor in heaven will be occupied by great servants—those who walked on this earth in humility, like Moses. I'm not asking God for a place of honor, but I am asking Him to help me become a better servant. I'm asking Him to create in me a deeper passion for others, and that I would learn how to take the place of a servant.

What is your prayer right now? Write it out.

Of course, we don't know what kind of servant Joshua was, but this next passage just might give us a little more information. Read **Exodus 33:7-11** and summarize briefly.

The Tent of Meeting was the first stationary place where God came down to meet with Moses. It was before the erection of the Tabernacle. But what stood out to me is that Joshua was a young servant and he never left the Tent.

Why do you think he stayed there?

Let's think about this for a minute. Joshua witnessed spectacular things in this place. Moses may have been the one that God spoke to, but Joshua saw the pillar—or the presence of God—with his eyes and he heard the voice of God. Don't you wish you could have been present for at least one of these encounters? This was the holiness and majesty of God displaying great movement right before their eyes. And Joshua was a young student just taking it all in.

How did Moses speak to God (**Exodus 33:11**)?

Since God is spirit and Moses learns that he cannot look upon God's face and live (**Exodus 33:20**), we can take this phrase *face-to-face* to mean "intimately." Hence, God and Moses were friends.

Think of a good friend. What do you enjoy about that friendship? Is it easy? Is it fun? Can you talk about anything? Describe this friendship.

Yesterday I went to church with my dear friend, Michelle. As we walked through the hallway, she introduced me to this beautiful lady. Michelle's friend wanted me to know that Michelle is one of her very best friends. I said to her, "Well, she's my BFF." She then looked at me and said, "She's my *double* BFF." We laughed. Here's the great thing about my friendship with Michelle: it's easy. I can be myself without fear of judgement. There's no jealousy. There is never a lull in our conversation as we always have stuff to talk about. We have so much fun together. And the most important thing is we have one common denominator: Jesus Christ.

Here's what I know. I want my friendship with Jesus to be even better than the ones I share with intimate friends. I want to talk face-to-face with Jesus, like Moses talked to his Father.

What did Jesus pray for in **John 17:11**?

Will you strive for this kind of intimacy with Jesus? How?

Let's quickly return to our story in **Exodus 33**. What do you think Joshua learned about God in the Tent of Meeting?

How do you think it prepared him for his future work?

The pillar of cloud represented the presence of God. Obviously, Moses and Joshua learned that God was always with them and that He would lead them every step of the way—through the wilderness and on into the Promised Land. Imagine how this impacted a young man who would one day succeed Moses. Just imagine…

Do you see yourself in this story? How?

Day 5

The Faith of a Warrior

Today we examine a passage that, in my mind, is one of the most moving stories in all of Scripture. Not only does it show the dark side of unbelief, but it also illuminates the glorious result of faith.

Begin by reading **Numbers 13:1-16**.

Who is the one that sent the spies (**verses 1-2**)?

Now here's an interesting part to this command. What do you learn from **Deuteronomy 1:21-25**?

Why would they do this? They had God's promise that He would deliver them into the Promised Land and they witnessed unbelievable miracles along the way. So why wouldn't they just trust God? Well, here's what I think. It's easier to walk by sight than to walk by faith. In any case, this is surely the beginning of their downfall. They may have fared better had they just trusted God instead of asking to go scope out the land.

How are we supposed to live, according to **2 Corinthians 5:7**?

If you would like to examine your faith further and learn to walk by faith, then you should consider working through my *Fearless Faith Bible study*. It may change your life.

Look back at **Numbers 13:1-3**. What men were chosen to explore the land?

As we move on, take in mind that these men were leaders, respected members of the Israelites. This is important to note as we'll soon see their influence among the people.

Read **Numbers 13:17-20**. On their journey to spy out the land, what were they to do? Write down specifics.

Summarize **Numbers 13:21-25**.

Compare **Exodus 3:8** with the previous passage. Would you say that the land was as God had promised? Explain.

It's important we look at the spies in this next passage. Remember, there were twelve explorers. As you read **Numbers 13:26 –14:10**, compare what you learn about the ten spies with Joshua and Caleb.

Ten spies:

Joshua and Caleb:

Now before we shake our heads in disbelief and wonder how ten of the spies could come back with such a bleak picture, I'm thinking that we might have sided with them as well. In fact, I see this as a big problem in the church today. It is easier to walk by sight than it is to walk by faith. If we can't see what's ahead, or we don't know the outcome, then we just don't want any part of it. If it seems like a daunting task and we don't believe we are qualified, then we often choose the easier road. But here's the thing: when God is in it and it's His plan for our life, then it usually goes way beyond our comfort zone. He rarely gives us all the details and never sheds light on the outcome. All He asks is that we trust Him and walk with Him.

The Israelites had incredible miracles to look back on. We have the completed Scriptures at our disposal. The Israelites had God's promise. We, too, have God's promises. So in my estimation, walking by faith is a no-brainer. Walking by faith shows God that we trust Him and we believe He will get us through. I heard it said that "the WILL OF GOD will never take you to a place that the GRACE OF GOD won't bring you through." Oh, how true this is.

Is God asking you to do something and you've been hesitating? What will you do?

Returning to our story at hand, I see this bad report/good report as a *focus* issue. The ten spies focused on the people, their size and strength. They saw giants. Caleb and Joshua saw the same things, but they focused on God. They knew that God was bigger, He had promised, and He would give them the land.

Who had the most influence on the community (**Numbers 14:1-4**)? What happened?

It only takes one or two people to stir up a crowd. In this case, it was ten leaders. Their strong negativity was so convincing that the whole community grumbled in disbelief. If you are a believer, then you are a leader. And it is our responsibility to lead people *to* God, not away from Him. Therefore, we need to be careful how we react in certain situations, what we say, and what we do. Negativity spreads fast. We are not expected to be perfect—that's impossible—but God wants us to reflect Him in everything. Let's choose to walk like Caleb and Joshua even if it goes against the crowd.

Earlier I said that this story reflects the dark side of unbelief, but it also illuminates the glorious result of faith. Let's look at these together. Write down your findings below:

The dark side of unbelief (**Numbers 14:20-37**):

The glorious result of faith (**Numbers 14:24, 38**):

Their unbelief caused them to wander aimlessly in the desert for forty more years, and it excluded them from entering the land. Every person that exited Egypt twenty years and older died in the desert, except Joshua and Caleb. Imagine how many graves were dug. The freedom they thought they had won quickly turned into confinement. Oh, the dark side of unbelief.

Write out **Numbers 14:24**:

This verse is tucked in the middle of such dark stuff that we could easily miss it. My heart was moved when I read what God said about Caleb. I want the same kind of spirit as him. Do you? Will you join me and pray that God would give us a spirit that follows Him wholeheartedly? Without a doubt, this is the kind of heart God looks for and the kind that brings honor to Him. Let's not follow the crowds—the crowds of people who are not following God—even if they *are* believers. Let's seek to honor Him. Let's choose to walk by faith.

Skim through Days 1-5 and write down what you learned about Joshua. How do you think these details prepared him to become one of heaven's mightiest warriors?

We are off to a good start. There's so much more we need to learn, but I trust that you already have a good handle on what God looks for in a warrior. It's not about how well we fight, but it's about letting *God* fight for us. Remember that our God is bigger than the toughest opponent. Let's stay engaged and ready.

---

1. http://cnsnews.com/blog/michael-w-chapman/billy-grahams-daughter-2016-enemy-advancing-darkness-evil-permeating-our
2. *Holman Bible Dictionary* (Nashville, TN: Holman Bible Publishers, 1991), 816-817.
3. LOGOS: Wiersbe's Expository Outlines of the Old Testament.

Week 2
A Warrior Set Apart

Day 1
The Commissioning
Day 2
Taking the Reins
Day 3
Great Instruction
Day 4
Spiritual Chain of Command
Day 5
An Unlikely Heroine

I've heard many believers say that they have trouble grasping the Old Testament. They would much rather study the New Testament. I understand what they are saying, but it is always my goal to help Bible students gain deep truths from the Old Testament. I long for them to see how the *whole* Bible fits together. If we only had the New Testament, we would never see God's redemptive plan unfolded. Hence, the Bible is complete with sixty-six books—thirty-nine books in the Old Testament and twenty-seven books in the New Testament.

Jesus said, **"I tell you the truth, until heaven and earth disappear, not the smallest letter, not the least stroke of a pen, will by any means disappear from the Law until everything is accomplished" (Matthew 5:18).** This tells me that the whole counsel of God's Word is important, not just the parts we find easy to understand.

I hope you have determined to go all the way in this study. I will try and bring life to every story, situation, and divine occurrence. I believe we will find many truths relational to the Church and to our lives. While Joshua and the Israelites moved forward with God's plan centuries ago, we can move forward today as we study God's Word.

This week we examine a warrior set apart. Joshua was set apart from the rest for a greater work. We need to remember that he was human just like us. And while he was trained, I wonder if he felt ready when the call finally came. I wonder if he felt inadequate to step into Moses' shoes. Maybe he bargained with God. We really don't know, but it's important to note that Joshua was *chosen* by God. He could never have accomplished such amazing feats without being set apart and divinely positioned for such a task. I'm excited to advance with Joshua. I trust God will ignite our hearts on fire and that we'll have plenty of truth to hold on to.

Day 1
The Commissioning

Before we advance into the book of Joshua, we need to examine one more important piece to this divinely orchestrated puzzle. Today we will spend the majority of our time in the book of Deuteronomy. This Old Testament book of the Bible is perfectly positioned between the forty-year wilderness wanderings and the entrance into the Israelites' new land.

The desert living was coming to a close and God had buried a whole generation of people. As Moses gathered the nation before him **(Deuteronomy 1:3)**, a new generation had sprung up. These would be the ones to capture God's promise—the promise of the land He had prepared them for.

What was the purpose of this gathering, according to **Deuteronomy 1:3**?

As Moses spoke to the people, he knew it would be his last message. He also knew that he would *not* be the one to lead the people into the land. Why? Well some time back, he disobeyed God. He was instructed to speak to the rock so the people could drink, but instead, he hit the rock because he was annoyed and angry with their never-ending complaining and arguing **(Numbers 20:1-12)**. God then said to Moses, **"Because you did not trust in me enough to honor me as holy in the sight of the Israelites, you will not bring this community into the land I give them" (Numbers 20:12).**

I used to feel sorry for Moses, but today I read it with new insight. He had many years under his belt as a leader. And leading God's people was *never* easy. In fact, it was grueling at times. While there are always consequences to sin, something tells me that God had prepared Moses. He *would* enter the Promised Land, but not the one on the earth. The Land he would enter would be so much grander. When my sister was diagnosed with cancer, she fought with everything inside her. She was a young forty-three at the time. In the end, though, it was obvious that God had prepared her for death. She was ready to meet Jesus.

I think Moses was ready, too. God had prepared him. And he joyfully finished the task God had given him as he stood before the people on this day. God moved his heart as he spoke. It was a long message, but a message filled with instruction on what God commanded of the people once they became owners of this new place. The struggles of the desert would be behind them, and the fruitfulness of the new land before them. God simply didn't want them to forget all He had done for them and fall into apathy and complacency. He was the One to be worshiped, not foreign idols. So Moses spoke what God told him to say.

Why do you think God chose this moment—the moment they stood on the brink of their new land—to speak these words?

Do you think we are closer to God when things are going well, or when our circumstances are daunting? Explain using a personal example.

Read **Deuteronomy 32:44-47**. How important was this message Moses delivered?

Does this give you any idea how important the Word of God is? Based on what you read, what should be our response to God's commands?

Now let's move forward with our topic—the commissioning of Joshua.

Read **Numbers 27:15-23**. Write down the events of Joshua's commissioning.

A great leader is one who cares about his flock and does not seek self-glorification. Moses exemplifies this kind of leader. Rather than wallow in self-pity because he was kept from entering the land, his concern was for the people of Israel. He wanted them to have a righteous leader—a leader who would lead them the way he had done. He did not want the flock of God wandering aimlessly without a shepherd. So he boldly and humbly asked God to name a successor.

And Joshua was chosen!

From what you've studied so far, why do you think Joshua was a good candidate to lead the people?

I imagine Moses was thrilled with God's selection. He knew Joshua since Joshua was young. He had watched him grow spiritually, intellectually, and physically. He observed the heart of a servant and the soul of a warrior. Joshua's love for God was unsurpassed and his faith unmeasured. There's nothing like witnessing someone you have mentored become an amazing asset for the kingdom of God. Perhaps Moses said to God, "Good choice!"

And Joshua was commissioned!

The Hebrew word for *commission* means "to command, order, instruct, and give instruction." The dictionary defines *commission* this way: "the act of committing or entrusting a person with supervisory power or authority."[1]

I've witnessed many people commissioned for God's work, mostly pastors and missionaries. They are brought before the congregation and prayed over. Witnessing this always moves my heart. Basically, the church is following biblical protocol. They are in essence giving their blessing and imparting authority to go into the world and do what God called them to do.

Thus, this is what we are witnessing with Joshua.

Why did God instruct Moses to give some of his authority to Joshua (**Numbers 27:20**)?

While the people often complained and griped under Moses' leadership, they still obeyed him. He walked with high integrity and spoke with authority from God. By imparting authority to Joshua, the people would obey him as well. The commissioning was a crucial facet to transferring leadership.

Write down everything you learn from the following passages:

Deuteronomy 1:37-38:

Deuteronomy 3:26-28:

Deuteronomy 31:14, 23:

God chose Joshua. And the commissioning made it official. Joshua would have authority and power just like his predecessor. He would lead God's people into their inherited land and govern the nation. He would become a strong leader and a powerful military general. We read at the end of Joshua that **"Israel served the LORD throughout the lifetime of Joshua and of the elders who outlived him and who had experienced everything the LORD had done for Israel" (Joshua 24:31).**

I want you to know that ALL believers have been commissioned, not just pastors, missionaries, and church leaders. Let's close our lesson today by looking at this.

Write down the commission Jesus uttered in **Matthew 28:18-20**. What does it involve?

On this mountain, Jesus passed His authority to the disciples who were present. In turn, they took the gospel as far as they could and equipped countless more disciples. Then they passed the authority to us. So my challenge to you today is to pour yourself into this commission and ask God if you are faithfully fulfilling it.

Write down your thoughts.

Day 2
Taking the Reins

Read **Joshua 1:1-5** and summarize briefly.

When did Joshua become the leader of Israel (**Joshua 1:1-2**)?

Joshua did not take the reins of leadership until after Moses had died. I found this interesting. This was the right timing and a perfect end to Moses' era. God let Moses finish out his duties before assigning the new leader. Therefore, Moses went down in heaven's chronicles as a highly esteemed leader. I'm certain that when the people looked back, they had highest regard for their former chief. And here's the best part: Moses' story has been recorded for all of us to read and emulate.

Sometimes people are in such a hurry to take over leadership, they step on others' toes to get there. Often pride and arrogance are the culprits that make them go ahead of God and push people aside. The sad reality is that this happens frequently in the church. So many times people get hurt because of leaders who choose selfish ambition rather than letting God lead them.

Our lesson today reminds us that it's important we let God put us in the position He chooses. And in His time.

Where is God placing you in the framework of the church? In ministry? Is He calling you into a specific leadership position? Are you waiting on Him? Go before God as you ponder this and write down what comes to your mind.

Write out **Joshua 1:2**.

In the previous verse, what stands out to you about God's ways?

In our previous lesson, we learned that the words in Deuteronomy were Moses' last before he died and before the people left the desert. What did God say to the people in **Deuteronomy 1:6-7 (NIV)**? Fill in the blanks:

"The LORD our God said to us at Horeb, 'You have _____ long enough at this mountain. Break camp and _____ into the hill country of the Amorites...'"

Throughout Scripture we notice one obvious thing about God: He is ALWAYS moving forward with new things. God may choose to keep things the same for a while, but then He decides to change things up a bit. He always has something new on the horizon. And in this case, He was going to deliver His people from the desert and bring them into a spacious and luxurious land. How exciting is that?

There's not a better lesson for us. Too many believers are content living in the past that they miss out on the new things God wants to do. I've witnessed many a pastor struggle when the people in his church balk at his new ideas. The congregants often cause havoc at every decision he tries to implement. They want things to remain the way they've always been. Sometimes they never come around. Eventually, the pastor feels depleted and the joy of ministry diminishes. All he wants to do is move his flock to better pasture with God, but instead, the resistance makes him feel like a failure.

Why do you think people are often hesitant to move forward?

What would be the advantage to moving ahead with God?

Ponder the scenario in **John 5:1-9**. Write down what this man's life may have been like after he met Jesus, and what it would have been like had he rejected Jesus' offer.

When Jesus walked into the pool area at Bethesda, he felt compassion for a particular man who had been lame for thirty-eight years. When Jesus approached the man, He asked, **"Do you want to get well" (verse 6)**? This question used to trouble me. I thought, "Of course, he wants to get well." But then again, he had been that way for a very long time. Perhaps he was comfortable as an invalid and fearful of a new way of life.

Thankfully this crippled man chose to accept Jesus' healing. Imagine how his life changed. He could now walk, skip, and run. He didn't have to beg any more. The quality of his life changed in a quick second. This is a perfect picture of what it means to move forward with God and not stay stuck in the past.

Is God opening up a new door for you? Is He asking you to move forward with Him? What will be your response? Write out your prayer.

Here's an important observation: a wise leader, while called to move forward, doesn't completely abandon the past, but builds on it. We will see this with Joshua. In fact, Moses is mentioned fifty-seven times in the book of Joshua.

Let's take a look. In what ways do you see Joshua building on Moses' legacy?

Joshua 4:10-12:

Joshua 8:30-35:

Joshua 17:4:

Joshua 20:1-3:

As you can see, Moses was not forgotten. Nor was the groundwork he laid out for the people. Joshua kept Moses' legacy alive long after his death. Therefore, Moses remained a revered leader. As Joshua took the reins, he would lead with diligence, strength and wisdom just like his predecessor. He would guide the people of Israel forward with God, but never abandoning the former principles and commands God gave through Moses.

What did God say to Joshua in **Joshua 1:5**?

Leaders need encouragement. It can be a lonely path sometimes. And it can also be stressful and tiring. We are responsible for the flock under our care and Christian leaders are the most in-demand people I know. If leaders don't protect their personal time, they can easily get sucked in until they're worn out spiritually, emotionally, and physically. I have faced it. Perhaps you have, too.

No doubt, Joshua would face some extremely difficult days ahead. His flock was huge and they had a reputation of unruly behavior sometimes. They were not always happy campers. He had leaders under him, but ultimately he was in charge of the masses. God knew this and so He encouraged him before he even started. Imagine how Joshua felt hearing these words. A good way to start a new position, wouldn't you agree?

Do you need encouragement today? If so, read through Joshua 1 and let God speak to you. Do you know a leader who needs encouragement? How will you encourage them?

What is your take-away from today's lesson? What will you apply to your life, your ministry?

Day 3
Great Instruction

Joshua is standing on the heels of greatness. He will witness spectacular things and be challenged in this new role. Since the Israelites left Egypt forty years prior, Joshua had known God's plan and promise. He heard the people speak of it. While God showed up in miraculous ways, the wilderness was still a hard and difficult time in the life of God's people. They survived on manna and quail every day, felt the dry heat of the desert against their skin, watched a whole generation die, and experienced God's judgement from outright disobedience. And now—as Joshua stared cautiously into the future—his beloved mentor was gone and he was left holding the reins.

I'm usually a wimp and cower at the thought of doing something big and outside my comfortable little area. But I also understand what it's like to have God's call on my life. No matter how scary the task seems, I just cannot say no. Jeremiah the prophet said: **"If I say, 'I will not mention him or speak any more in his name, his word is in my heart like a fire, a fire shut up in my bones. I am weary of holding it in; indeed, I cannot'"** (Jeremiah 20:9). Oh, the life of a prophet. Jeremiah must have wished for just one day of serenity instead of one filled with proclaiming messages of doom and gloom. But in the end, he couldn't hold it in. God had called him.

God had called Joshua, too. Scripture doesn't tell us what Joshua was going through when the time of usurping the leadership position was upon him. Perhaps he didn't tell a soul. But God knew. So, God gave him great encouragement and instruction.

Read **Joshua 1:6-9** and summarize God's word to Joshua.

When did God declare the land for His people, according to **Joshua 1:6**?

That's right! The inheritance was affirmed long before this day. In fact, it had been their land all along. It was promised to Abraham, Isaac and Jacob. For centuries God was moving His people toward the land. It didn't matter if the people occupying the land were bigger and stronger, or that they would never willingly leave. What mattered was that the people of Israel had to step out on faith and claim it.

Forty years before, they failed miserably. The crowd sided with the doubting spies. They refused to walk in faith. They let fear capture their hearts. So the desert became their home. But now a new leader rose to power. Joshua had lived through God's penalty for the people's disobedience. And he wasn't about to let that happen again. Perhaps on this day, Joshua exerted a faith he had never known before. He knew what he must do. He would lead the people into their new awaited land—the land flowing with milk and honey.

Can you picture this scene with me? What do you envision?

As we discussed earlier in our study, the land of milk and honey is symbolic of the land that awaits us. And the only way to claim it is through faith in Jesus Christ. Jesus promised us a fruitful life on this earth. He said, **"I have come that they may have life, and have it to the full" (John 10:10)**. But here's a stark reality: many believers have yet to live this way. They simply exist, living in survival mode. Friends, this is not the life Jesus came to give us. He's not offering us a life free of struggles, but He is promising us inner joy no matter the circumstances. This is freedom in Christ. This is abundant living. And like the Israelites, we need to step out on faith and claim it as our own.

What is the promise to believers in **Ephesians 1:3**?

Right now would be a good time to do a self-evaluation. Are you just existing? Or are you living the way Jesus described? Write down your thoughts and your plan of action.

Let's return to our passage, **Joshua 1:6-9**. God breaks down what *His* success is. Here's my two cents: this message is for *every* believer. We want to be successful, but we often look for it in the world. We work towards the approval of people when the only one who really matters is God. One day we'll be accountable to God. His opinion should be above all other opinions. God tells Joshua—and us—how we can be successful in His eyes and for His kingdom. So really ponder the remainder of today's lesson.

What does God tell Joshua (**Joshua 1:7**)? Fill in the blanks:

"Be _____ and very _____."

Now read the remainder of the verse. Where does strength and courage come from?

God doesn't expect His people to be strong and courageous on their own. That's not even possible, especially when it comes to accomplishing His work. God tells Joshua that he will become strong and courageous through the Word of God.

I must tell you that this is speaking to my heart right now. I have some upcoming engagements that are making me anxious. Today, though, God reminded me that I can be strong and courageous. I can draw everything I need from His Word.

How about you? Are you feeling weak right now? Unsuited for something coming up? Inadequate? Anxious? Write out what you are going through at this moment.

Now that we know where strength and courage come from, let's follow God's great instruction to Joshua and find out how we can get it.

Write down what you see as the strategy for God's success based on **Joshua 1:6-9**. Don't leave anything out.

Let's now discuss these things a little more and seek to apply them to our lives.

During the years leading God's people, Moses kept a written record of God's Word and acts and committed it to the priests **(Deuteronomy 31:9)**. So at the time of the conquest of the Promised Land, the people of Israel followed five books – *the Law* – that governed their lives. These are the first five books in our Bible. This was the Law God was referring to. But we live centuries later and possess the completed Scriptures. The Law for us would be the entire Bible.

How much of the law should we obey **(verse 7)**?

The word *all* in this verse is critical to our success. God doesn't want partial obey-ers. He wants *total* obey-ers. But we often pick and choose commands to obey and negate others. I know I've been guilty of doing this. The Bible is filled with commands, so it's important we study Scripture to find out if there are some we are ignoring.

What is your prayer?

The word *meditate* in **verse 8** means "to mutter." It was a practice of the Jews to read Scripture aloud **(Acts 8:26-40)** and to talk about it to themselves and to one another **(Deuteronomy 6:6-9)**.[2] This may be why God warned Joshua that the Book of the Law was not to depart from his mouth.

Compare **James 1:22-25** with "meditating" on the Law. What are we to do with God's Word?

What does the phrase "looks intently" in **verse 25** mean to you?

In referencing this phrase from **James 1:25**, Warren Wiersbe says that it means to gaze carefully, not glance casually.[3] I believe that "meditating" on God's Word is the same concept. Ponder it! Maybe look at other Bible versions. Read it carefully, always examining how it applies to your life.

Here are two more questions from our passage in Joshua:

What do you think God means when He says **"do not turn from it to the right or the left" (Joshua 1:7)**?

When are we to meditate on God's Word **(Joshua 1:8)**?

I know I want to please God and be successful for His kingdom work. Our forefathers, Joshua included, left us a lasting legacy. These are big shoes to fill. But if we follow this great instruction from Joshua 1, we can also be successful. Is this what you want?

Take a moment to write out what God spoke to you about as you worked through your lesson. How will you apply it to your life?

Day 4
Spiritual Chain of Command

This morning I read a blog on leadership. The author said, "I experience the greatest doubt and anxiety at the start of something big. Whether it's good or bad, I'm usually fine once I'm going. But until then, I'm like the person on the tip of the high dive, overlooking way too much blue." Oh, how I can relate.

Something tells me that Joshua was looking at the same blue. Yes, God's call was on his life. Yes, God gave him powerful promises to hold on to and great instruction to take with him. But he was still human and had never done anything like this before. However, he would move forward with butterflies in his stomach and sweat on his palms. As Joshua gets things ready for the big capture, his anxious heart would eventually turn into one of strength and courage.

Summarize in your own words **Joshua 1:10-18**.

As a reminder, read again **Joshua 1:10-11** and fill in the blanks:

"So Joshua ordered the officers of the people: 'Go through the camp and tell the people, _____ _____ _____ _____.'"

It is here where Joshua takes full command. He has now stepped into the shoes of Moses and begins a renowned leadership position. He begins by getting the people ready.

According to **Joshua 1:10**, who did Joshua speak to?

One of the best things that happened to Moses in the desert was when his father-in-law paid him a visit **(Exodus 18)**. It is definitely worth your time to read this chapter. When Jethro heard about all the good things God had done through Moses for His people—the miracles included—he came to the desert to meet with Moses. But during his visit, Jethro became troubled when he saw Moses serving as both judge and jury for all the people. Remember that one and half million people fled Egypt. Night and day Moses handled every problem, big and small.

So Jethro offered Moses some valuable advice that he was able to incorporate into his new leadership role. He instructed Moses to elect leaders from each tribe and teach the leaders how to handle the day-to-day things. The bigger issues could be brought to Moses. Moses listened to his father-in-law and did everything he told him to do. Hence, huge weights were lifted off Moses' shoulders.

Most likely these leadership positions (howbeit, different people) were still in place, and these are the leaders Joshua selected to help the people get ready.

Who was the leader of Joshua?

Who was the leader of the people?

Right here, we see the spiritual chain of command:

God → Joshua → the people

This spiritual chain of command should still be in place in the New Testament church.

Write out the spiritual chain of command for the church and the family based on **Ephesians 5:23-24.**

How does this speak to your life? What is God saying to you?

Jesus is the absolute authority for the church. The God-ordained leaders receive their instruction from Him, and they in turn guide the people. But far too often we see this chain of command broken because the people refuse to follow the leader. This happens in the church more than we think.

Summarize Paul's concern with the church at Corinth **(1 Corinthians 1:11-12)**?

Read further in this passage, **1 Corinthians 1:13-17**. What did Paul tell the leaders of this church?

Many things can empty the cross of its power **(1 Corinthians 1:17)** and division is positioned at the top of the list. At one time the Corinthian church was overflowing with truth. Their light was a bright beacon of hope in this bustling metropolitan center. But somewhere along the way, the church lost its focus. The enemy slipped in causing division and chaos. They were clearly divided in their allegiance. When the apostle Paul heard about it, he sent a letter to warn them. Paul explained that their behavior was hurting the cause of Christ instead of advancing it.

Have you seen such division in the church or in your personal life? What happened?

How do you think we can hinder the cross of Christ?

God set up a structure. And when that structure breaks down, the repercussions are insurmountable. This is true in any God-ordained institution: the church, marriage, the family, or government. It's important we respect those in leadership over us. We may not agree with them all the time, but we need to respect them.

Again, how did the people respond to Joshua's leadership position **(Joshua 1:16-18)**?

Now go back and read **Exodus 17:1-3**. Write down what happened.

As Joshua stands before this new generation of people, he remembers a day when the people weren't so compliant. Imagine how overjoyed he was to hear the peoples' response. Their yielding attitudes must have sent Joshua's spirit soaring.

Joshua is off to a good start and God is with him. No doubt, the Spirit of God was all over this and God was about to unleash great power. The people were compliant and ready to move forward with their new leader. Are you excited to move along with him as well?

Write out your thoughts as we conclude our lesson today.

Day 5
An Unlikely Heroine

Today's lesson is a story about an unlikely Old Testament heroine. A story with a lasting legacy. A winner by God's standards. I'm pretty sure that your heart will be moved, just like mine. I can't wait. Let's get going.

Begin by reading **Joshua 2:1-24**.

Good leaders will not back away from obstacles. They will find a way around them. They might remove them, climb over them, or walk around them. They are not afraid of road blocks. As Joshua begins to take the reins of leadership, he immediately encounters a HUGE obstacle — the heavily fortified city of Jericho. This walled-off city was the Israelites' way into the Promised Land, but it was also tightly shut up **(Joshua 6:1)**. Jericho covered about eight acres of land, with huge walls surrounding the city. The walls consisted of an inner wall and an outer wall. The inner wall was 12 feet thick, the outer wall was 6 feet thick, and the entire structure stood about 30 feet high. Needless to say, this would have been quite a challenge for *any* army to break through. But the army about to attack was no ordinary one because their God was BIGGER than any man-made structure.

Still, Joshua needed to know what they were up against. What did he do, according to **Joshua 2:1**?

Who came to the spies' aid **(Joshua 2:1)**?

What profession does **Joshua 2:1** attribute to Rahab?

Some commentators, to remove the dishonor of being a prostitute, say that Rahab may have been a tavern keeper. However, the Hebrew word *zanah* used for "prostitute" in our passage means "harlot." Indeed, Rahab was exactly that – a Canaanite prostitute who sold her body to men.

Rahab was certainly an unlikely candidate for God's redemptive purposes. In Week 4, we will learn more about this remarkable woman. But today, let's zero in on three characteristics Rahab demonstrates. Each one is important to understand what moves God's heart as Rahab is surely one of the greatest heroines of the Old Testament.

Rahab demonstrated…

1. Compelling *Courage*!

How do you see Rahab's courage played out in **Joshua 2:1-7**?

It would take a lot of courage to do what Rahab did. She risked everything to hide the spies on her roof under the flax. Flax was soaked in stagnant water and then laid out to dry. It must have been smelly and soggy, which is probably why the king's men didn't look for the spies there. Rahab must have wondered where such courage came from. No doubt, it was from God – the One she would later become acquainted with. It's also interesting that she was a prostitute. Under Israel law, her profession would have been grounds for death, but we don't know how Rahab's culture looked at such a profession. She may or may not have had friends. On this day, though, God's righteous character would collide with the sinful nature of a woman to accomplish His purposes.

What does this tell you about your God? How does this give you hope?

What does this passage show you about Rahab?

I see a woman with compelling courage. Courage like the lion in "The Wizard of Oz" at the end of his journey. Courage to stand and face her accusers. Courage that wouldn't let her back down. This would have been a perfect opportunity for her to look good in the eyes of her countrymen. If she turned the spies in to the authorities, perhaps they would give her high recognition. That surely would feel good after a lifetime of possible shame. Instead, she lied. Rather than identify herself with the heathen gods she was accustomed to, she identified herself with the people of a foreign God. She put the lives of these two strangers above her own comfort and security. She protected them from death. Evil would not rear its ugly head on this night. God prevailed in more ways than one.

Do you exert such courage when it comes to standing up for God? Or are you weak? Timid? Or scared to make a stand? Sometimes I find myself teetering on the fence. Should I or shouldn't I? Am I strong enough to withstand the backlash that often comes from speaking truth?

Today I read an inspiring true story. Several pastor's wives stepped out of their comfort zones and did what many in the church would balk at – they began a ministry in a strip club. They faced their fears and disregarded judgmental people as they ministered to the girls that worked in the club. Slowly the girls began to come around. These courageous pastors' wives witnessed God do unbelievable things. And it all started with a few women running hard after God. God can do the same with us if we are willing to venture outside our little bubbles and exert courage, just like Rahab did.

As I ponder this story about Rahab, the harlot from Jericho, I'm asking God to stir up a courageous spirit in me. I'm asking Him to help me step forward to do His work, even if it scares me. How about you? Will you do the same? Write out your prayer to God.

Rahab demonstrated…

2. Fearless *Faith*!

Read **Joshua 2:8-11** and answer the following questions:

What had the people of Jericho heard?

How did they react?

What did Rahab believe?

Write out Rabab's words in **Joshua 2:11**:

Compare Rahab's words with **Hebrews 11:6**. What does God honor?

Rahab's story is surely one that shows how God honors faith. She had a fearless faith – a faith not evident in anyone else in her city. Rahab may have been a sinful woman, but she exerted a deep faith in a God she did not know. She believed God would do everything He said He would.

Do you believe God at His Word? Do you believe He will take care of your situation today? How are you showing Him belief? Write out your response.

God's Word is gospel! It's more valuable than gold! It's higher than the highest mountain, deeper than the deepest ocean, and stronger than the strongest foe. In fact, the longest chapter in the Bible is about God's Word: **Psalm 119**. At your convenience, you may want to reflect on this marvelous chapter and write down everything you learn about God's Word.

Ponder **Psalm 19:7-11**, and then write out words and phrases describing God's Word.

How much do you believe these words? Do you believe God's precepts are right? Perfect? Trustworthy? Sure? If you do, then how will you respond in the midst of your difficulties right now? Will you trust God? Will you step out on faith even if it doesn't make sense? I'm sure that nothing made sense to Rahab, but she believed God at His Word. She did not have the completed Scriptures at her disposal, yet she believed. Not only do we have God's complete Word before us, but we also know Him. He is our God. Jesus is our Savior. And His Spirit lives in us. With that said, will you put your total faith in *your* God? Will you believe Him?

Rahab demonstrated...

3. Brave *Boldness*!

Summarize in your words **Joshua 2:12-24**.

It took brave boldness to ask the spies to save her life. She was a foreign woman with a past – a sordid past. She was a sinner still living in her sin. She knew the God of the Israelites to be holy. And she must have known that His people lived a far different lifestyle than her people. In spite of all the things against her, she still exercised boldness.

We see boldness throughout the Scriptures, especially in the New Testament church. The early believers seemed to face off with opponents at every juncture. In Acts 4, Peter and John were arrested and put in jail for preaching Jesus' resurrection. The authorities eventually released the apostles because of insufficient evidence. We read in **Acts 4:23** that **"On their release, Peter and John went back to their own people and reported all that the chief priests and elders had said to them."**

According to **Acts 4:24**, how did the people respond?

What did they pray for **(Acts 4:29)**?

I have missed many an opportunity to share Jesus with someone simply because I was too afraid. I've let precious opportunities go by because I wasn't bold enough to speak up. I know that God looks for boldness in His people. It takes boldness to speak His Name. So I will do what the early believers did – I'll pray for more boldness. How about you? Will you join me?

Rahab is certainly a role-model for all of us. In Week 4, we will watch God's favor poured out on her and her family, hear what the New Testament writers had to say about her, and uncover the place in redemptive history she retains – an uncanny heritage. So why is Rahab such an influential champion and why does her legacy live on? I believe it all goes back to what we learned today. These three things – courage, faith, and boldness – are fundamental elements to God's favor.

What principle(s) will you take away from today's lesson? How will you live it out?

1. http://dictionary.reference.com/browse/commission?s=t
2. LOGOS: Warren Wiersbe, *Be Strong*.
3. LOGOS: Wiersbe's Expository Outlines of the New Testament.

Week 3
Moving Forward

Day 1
Insurmountable Impasse
Day 2
Ark of the Covenant
Day 3
One Important Detail
Day 4
Crossing the Jordan
Day 5
Twelve Stones

What a privilege it is to continue with you in our study on Joshua. I trust you are enjoying the work, and that God is moving in your heart as He's showing you brand new things. One of the things we should always strive for is *maturity* in our faith. The writer of Hebrews says, **"Let us leave the elementary teachings about Christ and go on to maturity" (Hebrews 6:1).** But maturity comes at a cost. It takes discipline and the daily study of God's Word. How proud I am that you are on your way, Friends.

Have you ever been at a crossroads? An impasse? You were sailing along just fine and then you came to a screeching halt. A deadlock. No way forward. No way out. You shake your head in wonderment. Now what? How can I keep going? How can I move on? This is *not* how you envisioned your life playing out.

Guess what? This happened to the Israelites as well. God had promised them a land. A glorious land. They waited a very long time to get there. Forty years to be exact. Life was difficult for them in the desert. They were nomads living in a strange place. But then things began to look up for them. After years of breathing in desert dust and wandering the plains, Moses gave his final speech and Joshua became their new leader. God's promise was about to come to fruition. They would soon occupy the land God set aside for them.

But then the unthinkable happened. They came to an impasse. A huge obstacle. Call it what you like, but the fact remains; they were stuck. This week we will encounter a powerful God. A God that NEVER reneges on His promises. A God that is about to reveal His absolute glory and authority.

Join me as we move forward with God's people, their trusted warrior leader, and their God. Keep your eyes peeled and your heart engaged. We are about to witness unbelievable things. Things that just may catapult our faith to new heights.

Day 1
Insurmountable Impasse

I've been in ministry for almost thirty years, teaching and writing Bible studies for the majority of those years. And I've come to many roadblocks along the way. Impasses. More times than I can count, I've pictured myself standing on the banks of the Jordan River, seeing the destination in the distance, but wondering how I would cross to the other side without drowning.

Today the Israelites come to an impasse as well. Something tells me they weren't prepared for the difficulties before them or the miracles their God was about to hurl down from heaven. It will take great faith, unbelievable trust, and extraordinary courage to keep moving. Before you begin your study, take a moment and ask God to show up in the pages of Scripture and help you to see truths relevant to your life. Ask Him for fresh insight from a story that has surely made headlines down through the ages.

Have you ever been at a crossroads? A crossroads of faith? In his Bible study, *Experiencing God*, Henry Blackaby calls it a "crisis of belief." This is when a situation or experience brings you to a fork in the road. One path says, "I don't believe God at His Word." The other path says, "I believe what God has said." And you must choose which pathway to walk down. Will you walk by faith? Or will you walk by sight? Will you choose the easy road, or will you choose the harder one?

If you recall such a time, write it down and then record which pathway you took.

Our beloved group, the Israelites, just came to this place. Let's look and see.

First, recall again what God promised to His people **(Exodus 3:8)**.

How long before God's promise was to be fulfilled, according to **Numbers 32:13**?

After forty years of wandering in the wilderness, they are told that God is about to give them what He promised – a glorious new land. Read **Joshua 3:1** and **15**. Write down what they encountered next.

You've got to be kidding! Not only did God lead them to the banks of the fast flowing Jordan River, but it was early spring and the water was at flood stage. The melting snow from the nearby mountains, combined with the heavy winter rain, made the Jordan River a mile wide. This was NOT the time of year to attempt crossing the Jordan. What was God thinking?

Now imagine being in the sandals of the Israelites. Did they remember God's promise? Did they believe God at His word? Were their eyes focused on God, or were they focused on the deep water before them? What would they do?

Here's a simple assignment. Write out what you think the children of Israel could have done for each scenario:

Their eyes on the Jordan:

Their eyes on God:

What time-frame does Joshua give us **(Joshua 3:1-2)**?

It was ten miles from Shittim to the banks of the Jordan River [1] so I'm fairly certain that some of that time they were traveling. With so many people and their belongings, every movement took time. Imagine their reaction, though, once they got there. If we had been present, perhaps we would have heard all kinds of chatter. Those with weak faith may have voiced their worry and concern: How will we cross? We're going to die! Is God punishing us? There's NO way!

But without a doubt, there had to have been some with stronger faith. And they may have called corporate meetings to encourage the people: Remember what God did for us forty years ago. He parted the waters of the Red Sea so our people could walk on dry ground. They all made it safely to the other side. We *must* believe God. We *must* trust Him. He's got this under control.

What does **Romans 15:1-2** tell us about the strong believer vs. the weak believer?

In the introduction to this week's lesson, I mentioned that we should strive for maturity in our faith. The more mature we become, the stronger our faith will be. But sometimes we need someone strong to encourage *us*, especially if we doubt God's Word or we're struggling with an impasse we've come upon. Sometimes we need someone to remind us of God's promises, and that it's going to be okay. Within the body of Christ, there are many strong believers. Believers who exude an exemplary faith.

God will often bring us to an impasse – or a crossroads – to see what we'll do. If you're there right now and struggling to make sense of it, then search out someone strong in the faith. I did this the other day. I encountered a difficult situation and felt I needed to talk to someone else. I prayed about whom to contact and then I called the person God put on my heart. She offered valuable advice. She provided much-needed confirmation. Remember, too, that if you are strong in your faith, then you need to help weaker believers understand God's Word, especially when they are at a crossroads of faith.

What does **Jeremiah 6:16** reveal to you about your crossroad?

What does **Hebrews 11:6** mean to you? Do you see a correlation between these words and your impasse? What?

You may be asking yourself how you should proceed when you come to an impasse. How should you walk? Let's conclude today's lesson with three beneficial things we should put into practice before we take the next step.

When we are at an impasse, we should...

1. Walk on faith!

Ponder the following verse:

"For we walk by faith, not by sight" (2 Corinthians 5:7 ESV)

In relation to your impasse, what does this mean to you? How should you walk?

We may not understand God's purpose or His reason for something, but we need to trust that He is sovereign and in control. Walking by faith means that we will always obey the Bible, even when it rebels against our fleshly desires or our human reasoning. To walk by faith means that we will follow God no matter what, even when we can't see what's ahead. We need to trust God in every circumstance and live to bring glory to Him.

When we are at an impasse, we should...

2. Walk on what we know about God!

List 5 things you know about God. Support your answer with Scripture if you can.

1. _____
2. _____
3. _____
4. _____
5. _____

Choose one of the truths above and write down how it can help you in your impasse.

Early in ministry, I came to many crossroads of faith when asked to speak in public. Speaking is so outside my comfort zone that my flesh would sometimes scream. I looked at two paths before me. Path #1: *Yes*. Path #2: *No*. These were the days I struggled with intense fear and panic attacks. I knew I was called. I wanted to serve Jesus with my whole heart. But speak in public? Can't you think of something else, Lord? Something behind the scenes?

As I glared at both paths, I would search God's Word. I would focus on His character and His attributes. I would turn my attention to the miracles. God did some mighty acts in Scripture. I saturated my mind with what the Bible tells me about God. I chose to believe and walk in that. And without fail, God showed up in abundant ways. In the end, I'm so glad I walked on what I knew about God.

When we are at an impasse, we should...

3. Walk on every word that proceeds from the mouth of God!

What did Jesus say in **Matthew 4:4**?

What is your crossroad of faith right now? What does God say? List several key things He said that will guide you as you walk through it.

Do you truly believe God at His Word? **side note*: If you want to develop a strong and mighty faith, then consider working through my Bible study, *Fearless Faith: Doing Great Things for God*. You can find information on my website: www.solidtruthministries.com.

Day 2
Ark of the Covenant

In our previous lesson, we looked at three ways we are to walk when we come to an impasse. To review, write down what they are:

1. _____
2. _____
3. _____

Keep these in mind today as we observe another way we are to walk. And this one is vital to our success for God's kingdom work. I'm praying that you and I can grasp the importance of the Old Testament and that we'll see how the age-old practices really *do* help New Testament believers move forward with God. We have the privilege on this day to study a remarkable piece of furniture – the *Ark of the Covenant*.

Let's begin by observing a little history about the Ark of the Covenant.

Look up **Exodus 25:10-21**. Label the proponents to the ark.

Read the following passages. What do you learn about the Ark of the Covenant?

Exodus 25:22:

Exodus 26:30-34:

Exodus 40:1-3:

Leviticus 16:1-2:

We often think of the Israelites' wilderness years as a very dark time. No doubt it *was* difficult. The people had left the only country they knew, wandered for forty years, had to endure the awful desert weather, ate the same food day in and day out, and buried a whole nation of people. In addition, they were sitting ducks for their enemies with no walls to protect themselves. But if we could pinpoint one absolutely positive thing about the desert, it would be that God made Himself known to them. It is in the wilderness when God came to dwell among the people. He revealed Himself as a personal God – *their* personal God.

Moses was instructed to build a tabernacle, the place where God would meet with the people. The tabernacle was portable. Whenever the people picked up and moved on, they simply folded up the tabernacle and then reassembled it once they arrived in their new spot.

The Ark of the Covenant was the most valuable piece of furniture in the tabernacle. It represented <u>God's presence</u> and was the central focus of the Most Holy Place. The Ark of the Covenant was positioned behind a thick curtain, and the high priest would approach it *only* once a year (on the Day of Atonement) to make intercession for the sins of the people.

Our purpose today is to see how paramount the Ark was to Israel's journey into the Promised Land, and how significant it is to our lives.

Now that we've learned a little history, let's go back to Joshua. The Ark of the Covenant is the central theme of our story today.

Summarize **Joshua 3:2-4, 6**.

As the people stood on the banks, where was the Ark?

Look back at **Joshua 3:4**. Why was it important that the Ark go before the people?

Let's stop here and ponder this for a second. Remember that *all* of God's Word (Old and New Testament) is relational to our lives. The Ark of the Covenant represented God's presence. As the people begin their entrance into the land promised, God went before them. They would never have made it, found success, or been victorious without God leading the way. In fact, the conquering of the land would *never* have been possible without God at the helm. They needed to know which way to go and this was the only thing that made any sense.

How do you see yourself in this story?

How does it reflect what God wants from you?

What does **Joshua 3:4** tell us about the Ark and the people?

Does this give you any indication of how we should treat the presence of God?

The Ark of the Covenant was a *holy* piece of furniture. So holy that the people could not touch it (except the priests who carried it). Indeed, God's holiness is prevalent in the Old Testament. Our early fathers understood the holiness of God in relation to their own humanness. God was to be revered, worshiped, and adored.

I think the holiness of God has been lost in the Church. We come to God when it suits us. We bow to Him when it's convenient. We fail to bring our sin to Him. We ignore true repentance. We forget that God is the same yesterday, today and forever. He is *still* holy. Therefore, His people should treat Him with reverence. We will discuss this in more detail in our next lesson, but at least try to wrap your mind around the holiness of God for a second.

How are we instructed to behave, according to **1 Peter 1:15**?

Now study the next verse, **1 Peter 1:16**. Why are we to behave this way?

Write down ways you can apply this to your life.

For a minute, let's go back to the position of the Ark. Let me remind you that the Ark of the Covenant – the presence of God – went *before* the people. This was not up for debate. God said it! So they must follow if they were to claim the land and honor God.

Read **Matthew 4:18-19**. What did Jesus request of the two brothers?

Obviously this command is for us, too. And I believe that we should follow in *every* area of our lives. But what does that look like for you and me? Let's close with a simple assignment. Go through the following list and write out how you can follow Jesus in each particular area. Be sure to pray before writing your answers.

Marriage:

Parenting:

Family relationships:

Ministry:

Friendships:

Work:

Decisions:

Other _____:

Day 3
One Important Detail

It doesn't take Joshua very long to prove that he's appointed by God and a great commander in chief. There are many resources on the market today that teach us how to be good leaders. But none better than watching Joshua, heaven's mighty warrior, in action. Biblical leadership is ultimately about God – responding to God and then passing what you learn on to others. The backdrop for today's lesson comes from one verse: **Joshua 3:5**.

Summarize **Joshua 3:5**:

Based on what you've seen so far in our study, what makes Joshua a great leader?

Observe the sequence in this verse. Finish each section:

Joshua _____,

"Consecrate _____,

for tomorrow the LORD will _____."

I want to address each of these sections today so that you and I can see the progression and how they feed into the other. At the conclusion of each section, I've summarized it with one sentence.

Joshua told the people…

Remember what God said to Joshua after he was selected as the next leader? Read again **Joshua 1:7-8** and write down the instructions in a few words.

Being a biblical leader means that God is our highest and most valuable resource. Consulting outside resources is always good, but the Word of God should remain our top source.

What qualities should a good leader aspire to, according to **Hebrews 13:7**?

Author and pastor John Maxwell said, "A leader is one who *knows* the way, *goes* the way, and *shows* the way."[2] Certainly Joshua fits this description. Joshua listened to God and followed His instruction, whether it was popular or not. God said it! Joshua relayed it! And he led the way. Joshua obeyed God. Perhaps God chose him for such a time because the "once-rebellious" nation needed a leader who followed God, led with integrity, and spoke with authority. Surely the Church would be much stronger and healthier if every Christian leader followed this example.

Do you know a Christian leader who exemplifies this kind of leadership? Write down what you have learned from him or her and how they have impacted your life.

What principle does Joshua – or the leader you just mentioned – inspire you to incorporate into a particular area of your life? How will you do it?

Summary: A good leader is one who takes orders from God and acts upon them.

Consecrate yourselves...

Take some time to ponder **Joshua 3:5**. Why were the people to be consecrated?

Consecration wasn't a new concept for the people of Israel. What was the instruction Moses gave to the people in **Exodus 19:10-11**? Why did they do what they did?

In both instances (Joshua and Exodus), you may have noticed that God was about to do something really big. He was about to show up and reveal Himself. A great manifestation of His glory. Therefore, the people needed to be ready or they would miss the experience of seeing His majesty and splendor.

Have you ever missed something really awesome because you weren't there? What was it and how did it make you feel to only hear about it?

Biblical consecration has several meanings: 1) Set apart, to be holy; 2) Personal repentance of sin; 3) Putting oneself on spiritual alert to see God at work.

Remember that the people were getting ready for battle. I find it interesting that Joshua didn't tell them to sharpen their swords, check their equipment, or get their armor ready. No! He told them to consecrate themselves. This was God's battle. And if they really wanted to experience the power of God and watch Him work, then their hearts needed to be pure and undefiled. And consecration was the way to do it.

What a powerful word for us. We often get ready for battle our own way, with weapons we have at our disposal – human weapons. We use words, silence, arguments, anger, manipulation, and gossip. We choose to fight the battle, rather than let God do it for us. We ignore God's Word.

While consecration is an Old Testament word, the principle is still in effect for New Testament life. Compare **Colossians 3:5-10** with consecration. Ponder the list and write down any that may be prevalent in your life. What will you do to purify yourself?

How can you get ready for battle?

Summary: Consecration sets us up to see God's mighty works.

...for tomorrow the LORD will do amazing things among you.

I have read some amazing books, but there isn't a book more exciting and awe-inspiring than the Bible – God's Word. It is filled with intrigue, mystery, treasures, diversion, and fascinating people. It's also powerful, inspiring, convicting, encouraging, and life-changing. You know what else? The Bible is the *one* place where God truly manifests Himself – where He reveals His glory in great splendor and majesty.

And we are about to embark upon one of the most intense places in the Bible where God shows up. God will show His people who He really is. God will unleash great strength so the people will *never* forget. This manifestation will set the stage for the entrance into their new land. No doubt, the people will marvel at their God, His unlimited power, and His faithfulness.

In preparation for conquering the land we learned this week that the people needed to be ready. They would be consecrated. I pray that you and I will experience our God, too. I pray that we will stand in awe at the unveiling. Take a moment to prepare your heart right now, right where you are.

Summary: God delights in revealing Himself to His people

Day 4
Crossing the Jordan

The people have come a long way for this moment. Survival in the desert was difficult. But something tells me they haven't slept much the last few nights. Excitement is brewing. Anticipation is in the air. God is about to do something spectacular. Their eyes are open as they wait. Imagine a couple million people camped on the banks of the Jordan River waiting for instruction. They talk among themselves. Kids scurry around restless, but never venturing too far from mom and dad. Oh the noise *and* the smell of all the animals.

If you've been in ministry, you know that Satan always shows up just before God is about to do something big. Maybe he can hear the stirring in heaven and the angels shuffling around getting things ready. Perhaps he can sense that heaven is about to descend upon this place in an earth-shattering event. In any case, Satan is *not* pleased that God's people will forever be changed by the movement of God. So he comes in full force. He lies. He deceives. He causes confusion and doubt. And he wreaks havoc. I know you've seen it. I have, too. It's happened time and again in my life.

You would think Satan would know by now that he has no power to thwart God's plans. The psalmist said, **"But the plans of the LORD stand firm forever, the purposes of his heart through all generations" (Psalm 33:11).** You would think the devil would back down. But he never does. And according to Scripture, he never will until he is cast into the fiery furnace forever **(Revelation 20:10).**

Do you think Satan showed up in the crowd on this day? If so, what do you envision?

How can we recognize when Satan is trying to keep us from experiencing the movement of God?

After we recognize Satan's attempt at getting our eyes off God, what should we do?

As we move forward in our study, I want you to picture yourself among the people. Think outside the box and let your mind travel back to this moment in history when God is about to conquer the land He promised to His people.

Read **Joshua 3** and summarize.

What did God promise to Moses in **Exodus 33:14**?

How do you see this promise fulfilled in **Joshua 3**?

My husband jumped hurdles in high school. And I heard he was pretty good. Sometimes he knocked over the hurdles. Other times he scaled the hurdles and made it to the finish line without incident. I get out of breath just thinking about racing, let alone jumping over hurdles. I would rather sit in my comfy chair on the patio with a book drinking lemonade. Here's the thing: God's way is usually difficult and tiresome. And sometimes we have to jump hurdles along the way. *But God promises to always go with us.* Whatever road we walk, God goes before us.

According to **Joshua 3:13, 15-16**, when did the water stop flowing?

Imagine being one of those priests. Imagine hearing this instruction. I would think there might have been a few chuckles in the crowd. Or better yet, maybe some gasps. While the people were contemplating how they would cross the overflowing river, God had a plan. A plan they didn't understand, though. They must trust Him. This is a perfect picture of faith. The writer of Hebrews says, **"Faith is sure of what we hope for and certain of what we *do not see*" (Hebrews 1:1)**. And he goes on to say that **"this is what the ancients were commended for" (Hebrews 1:2)**. Perhaps the author had this story about the crossing of the Jordan fresh on his mind when he penned those words.

Has God ever given you instruction that you did not understand? You had no idea how you would ever do it. It seemed too inconceivable. Explain what it was and how you responded.

If you obeyed God and overcame your insecurities, what did you see God do in it all? Did it change your perspective of God? How?

At the Jordan River, what was the faith move that advanced the hand of God?

The people of God are about to enter into conflict to conquer the land. Success would *never* be possible without God going before them. Conflict often precedes conquest. The priests were to step into the water and get their feet wet. That's all. And God would do the rest. A true act of faith! No doubt God honors such acts of faith.

Unless we step out by faith and get our "feet wet," we're not likely to make much progress in living for Christ and serving Him. God usually asks us to step outside of our comfort zones for His kingdom work. Otherwise we would never learn how to depend on Him. Remember, faith is what *pleases* Him.

Write out **2 Corinthians 5:7**:

God doesn't expect us to understand, but He does expect us to obey even if we can't physically see what's before us. But how can we? Putting our faith and trust into something we cannot look upon or understand is so very hard. Well, here's the thing: God has given us a whole book filled with "faith" stories. And every time the people trusted God, the heavens roared with thunder. Can you see the smile on God's face when one of His children say "yes" and walk out on faith? If you are faced with an insurmountable task before you – something God is asking you to do – then take a moment and read a "faith" story in the Bible. It's sure to get you to move in the right direction.

What has God put on your heart lately? How will you respond?

The picture before us in **Joshua 3** is beautiful. From the following verses, write down where the Ark of the Covenant (God's presence) was positioned:

Joshua 3:8, 11:

Joshua 3:17:

Joshua 4:10-11:

How would you compare **Psalm 139:5** with what you saw in **Joshua 3**?

People often celebrate love, especially on Valentine's Day. Here's a truth we cannot dispute: we all need to be loved, but we'll never experience *true* love until we embrace the love of our Heavenly Father. There are many ways God shows us His love, but none more clearly than through His presence. Picture the scene before us in **Joshua 3**: God goes before the people into the Jordan River, stands in the middle of the people as they pass by, and then comes behind them once they've crossed. They are *never* alone. And you are never alone either.

One verse I love to ponder is **Zephaniah 3:17**: **"The LORD your God is with you, he is mighty to save. He will take great delight in you, he will quiet you with his love, he will rejoice over you with singing."**

From the previous verse, underline any words or phrases that jump out at you. Now write them down and next to each one, describe what it means. What is it like to have God's presence with you everywhere you go?

We just witnessed the first of several awesome miracles in the conquering of the land. But this is just the tip of the iceberg. As the people walked on faith and trusted God, He opened up a mighty pathway. What an awesome journey so far. We have lots more ground to cover, so hang in there with me. You'll be so glad you did.

Day 5
Twelve Stones

The nation of Israel is always on the move. But they are *not* going in just any direction. Have you noticed that they are moving forward, not backwards? Here's something we need to remember: we never stand still in the Christian life. We either move forward in faith or backward in unbelief. I think the people of God should serve as a strong example for us. Like Israel, we should always put one foot in front of the other and move forward.

What does it mean for you to be moving forward? Explain.

Which way are you going right now? Look at your circumstances and evaluate what direction you are heading. Write down how you might change the direction if you're heading the wrong way.

I just spent some time watching videos of powerful testimonies. These are stories of people who have been redeemed by the blood of Jesus, delivered from a life of sin, despair, and emptiness. Listening to amazing God-stories always revs up my spirit and rekindles a fire deep inside.

Imagine how peoples' lives were transformed when they heard testimonies from those who saw Jesus after His resurrection. Imagine what they heard. I saw Him! I saw the nail scars in His hands. Oh my goodness, His eyes radiated such joy. He put His hand on my shoulder – it was strong and tender. I'll never forget the look in His eyes when He stood in front of me – a look of deep love and gentle compassion. HE IS ALIVE!

Testimonies always seem to draw us in and cause us to believe. Why? Simply because the person telling the story witnessed it. Eye-witness accounts. God-testimonies are stories that show the greatness of God.

We have one more event to unfold before we can move forward with the nation to conquer the land. This will be a sign for future generations – a way to remember what God did for His people.

Read **Joshua 4** and summarize briefly.

Let's pull out pertinent information in this chapter. Answer the following questions:

What did the twelve stones represent **(verse 2)**?

What were the stones for **(verses 6-7)**?

What were the people to tell future generations when they asked about the stones **(verses 21-23)**?

What was the purpose of this memorial **(verse 24)**?

Fast forward a couple generations. A family is traveling through Gilgal on their way back home from Jerusalem. They walk past the pillar of stones. The son stops to take it all in. And then he asks his father, "Papa, what are these stones for?" With a smile on his face and a hand on his son's shoulder, his father says, "I'm glad you asked, Son. You see, many years ago our people were on the verge of redeeming our land but as they got closer to Jericho, they needed to cross the fast flowing Jordan River. With the Ark of the Covenant before them, God parted the water (it just stopped flowing) and they walked across on dry ground. God led them safely to the other side."

By this time, the son's eyes are about as wide as saucers. "Really? Is that true?" "Yes it is, Son," the father answers. "God is always faithful to His people. He leads us by the hand." And right there in front of the mound of stones, the family falls to their knees and worships Jehovah God.

Several years ago the metro Detroit area hosted a campaign to share the gospel. It was called EACH (Everyone A Chance to Hear). Five hundred churches and ministries jumped on board and for 6 months, we prayed, we trained, we gathered together, and we shared the gospel. I'm not sure that the Detroit area has ever experienced such powerful revival as we did during the EACH Campaign.

We heard amazing testimonies. One particular night a man from Ethiopia took the stage to share his story. Everyone was mesmerized as he talked about the demon-worshiping village he grew up in. His dad was one of the leaders. This was a testimony about angels coming to his house, two men showing up to share the gospel, his dad accepting Jesus Christ as his Lord, and that very night, the whole village (about 400 people) embracing Jesus and renouncing demons.

The story went on. His dad was illiterate – he never learned to read or write. Shortly after he accepted Christ as his Savior, he found a New Testament lying in the road. Not knowing where it came from, he opened it up and heard a voice say, "This is My Word." Sitting down under a tree with the Bible on his lap, he asked God to help him read it. Sure enough God opened up the pages of Scripture so that he could read it. For the next thirty-seven years (until his death), he could read the Bible, but nothing else. A true miracle!

I went home that night with a new vision of my God seared into my heart. This man's story catapulted my faith. It seemed God had revealed something about Him that I was vague on – His absolute power.

Imagine the faces of those hearing the story about God parting the waters. Imagine how that story catapulted their faith. No wonder God erected a memorial. God must have been so pleased every time He heard the story repeated.

It's always good to remember. Especially the things God has done for us. So let's do that right now. Below is a memorial of twelve stones similar to the one God's people erected outside Jericho. Take a few moments and list things that God has done for you. You might want to include truths from Scripture as well as personal things.

Remembering...

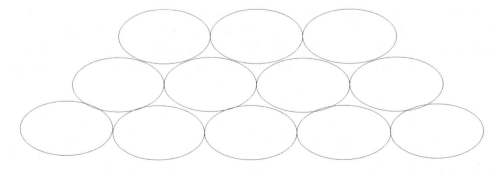

Now, take a moment to write a note to God thanking Him for all that He's done for you.

Dear God...

What is the admonition in **Deuteronomy 6:5-9**? List everything.

Does this admonition in Deuteronomy correlate with our passage in Joshua? How?

Why is it important to always remember what God did for you? Why is it important that we tell our children and others about it as well?

The world is a scary place right now and even scarier for parents raising children. But our children, grandchildren, and young people are the next generation to do the kingdom work. Sin is prevalent, the enemy lurks about, and kids are confused about so many things. That's why it's important we train them up knowing God's Word and teach them to embrace and defend truth. Tell them about the greatness of your God. To do that, we need to keep remembering what God has done for us. We need to immerse ourselves in God's Word and pray for them.

Let me encourage you to take those twelve things you carved into the stones and write them on note cards. Then place the note cards in a place you will see them every day. Recite them again and again so that you will be in the practice of remembering.

We come to the conclusion of Week 3. Thank you for hanging in there with me. Next week we move forward with the Israelites as they witness God do amazing feats to conquer the city He promised to them. Something tells me that our eyes will be awakened to even greater things.

---

1. LOGOS: Warren Wiersbe, *Be Strong*.
2. https://www.brainyquote.com/authors/john_c_maxwell

Week 4
Conquering Jericho

Day 1
Circumcision and Celebration
Day 2
The Commander's Appearance
Day 3
God's Battle Plan
Day 4
Redemptive Purposes
Day 5
A Fatal Mistake

You've prayed for a loved one. A friend. A situation. A job. A ministry. A health concern. A move. I've prayed, too. Hopefully you and I are praying people. But one thing that we learn early on is that when God answers those prayers, they may not – and probably won't – look like what we envision. God says, **"As the heavens are higher than the earth, so are my ways higher than your ways and my thoughts than your thoughts" (Isaiah 55:9)**.

That's right! God's ways are not only different than our ways, but they're so much better. Let me challenge you to go back and look at how God has answered some of your prayers. Something tells me that you will be in awe of how God orchestrated everything. At the time, you may have questioned God, or perhaps doubted His answer. But what did you gain from it? More trust? Increased devotion? Awakened heart? Deeper belief? Profound understanding? Gentle patience? Remember that God does things exactly the way He wants *and* for a glorious purpose.

Our lesson this week reveals a glorious purpose. The Israelites are standing on the outskirts of their new land. They're excited, nervous. They wonder. Taking the land won't be easy as they look into the face of huge obstacles. But God has a plan! An awesome battle plan! Still, it isn't what they envision. God is up to something *really* BIG. He is in control. They must trust Him. They must follow His direction. They must obey Joshua's orders. Heaven is about to converge upon this tightly closed up city of Jericho.

I want you to approach this week's lesson with your eyes wide open. Ask God to rally your heart and reveal amazing truths to you. Now, let's get going and see what God is up to.

Day 1
Circumcision and Celebration

If you are familiar with the early days of the Israelites' exodus from Egypt, you'll remember that the people were not very obedient when they embarked upon the desert. They complained and stood against Moses on multiple occasions. They wanted to go back to Egypt **(Numbers 14:3-4)**, even though in Egypt they were in a foreign land and subjected to slavery and harsh labor. Their disobedience culminated when they didn't believe God would give them the Promised Land – the land occupied by pagan people **(Numbers 13:31-33)**.

As Deuteronomy gives way to Joshua, the generation that came out of Egypt has died, and now a whole new nation of people has surfaced. This new nation seems to be much more obedient, don't you agree?

Why do you think they are more obedient?

It's a good thing when we learn from our mistakes, or the mistakes of our ancestors. Perhaps God's people had learned from their parents and grandparents mistakes? Or maybe the difficulties of living in the desert and the hope of a new land caused their hearts to soar with gratitude. No matter the reason, this new generation seems to be much more compliant and willing to move forward with God.

Is God moving in your life? Is He pulling you in a new direction? Is He tugging you away from the old that He might give you something new? How will you respond? Will you be like the first generation of Israelites (who grumbled), or the second generation (who obeyed)? Write out your answer.

Read **Joshua 5:1-12** and summarize in a few sentences.

What did the kings of Canaan hear about God **(5:1)**?

How did they react **(5:1)**?

What a blessing it is to have God on our side, rather than against us. The apostle Paul proposes a profound question: **"If God is for us, who can be against us" (Romans 8:31)**? He then goes on and asks another soul-searching question: **"Who will bring any charge against those whom God has chosen" (Romans 8:33)**?

Let me tell you that you are chosen by God if you've accepted Him as your Lord and Savior. John says, **"Yet to all who received him, to those who believed in his name, he gave the right to become children of God" (John 1:12)**. Therefore, you've been chosen.

Based on the truths in **Romans 8**, fill in the blank with your own word:

And all the people said _____!

You may have written the word *amen* in the blank. I did, too. Amen means "it is so!" We say amen when we feel deeply passionate about something. When I hear, **"If God is for us, who can be against us,"** I want to scream amen at the top of my lungs. There's not a better way to affirm truth.

I'm glad I will never know what it's like having God against me. But these foreign kings will find out exactly what that's like. Today the Israelites are camped not far from Jericho and God is going to prepare them for the battle at hand. We will look at what God does and then relate it to our lives.

While the Amorite kings west of the Jordan and all the Canaanite kings along the coast cowered in fear **(Joshua 5:1)**, what instruction did God give to Joshua **(Joshua 5:2)**?

To understand circumcision, we need to go back to Genesis. Circumcision was usually performed on babies or young Jewish boys and was a sign of their covenant relationship with God **(Genesis 17:10-11)**. It was God's way of *marking* His people and consecrating them as a holy people – a people set apart for the true and living God. Through circumcision, a person became a member of Israel's community and it provided them the right to participate in public worship. The outward sign of circumcision was to signify the inward change of heart.

How are you and I marked for God **(Ephesians 1:13-14)**? What is our sign?

What does it mean to you to be *marked* for God?

Look up **Colossians 2:11**. How did Christ circumcise you?

Let's quickly cover our passage before us. Why did God circumcise the men? Let me give you three reasons…

To restore their covenant relationship (Joshua 5:3-7)!

Israel is a covenant nation – a privilege God had given to no other nation **(Romans 9:4-5)**. This meant that the people were commanded to obey God. But when the people sinned against God in the wilderness (after their exodus from Egypt), God put a temporary hold on circumcision.

What does **Exodus 19:5-6** tell us about Israel?

The mark of the covenant meant that the people were to keep their bodies holy and not use them for sinful purposes. While they may have been tempted to sin in the wilderness, they would be more tempted in their new land – a land surrounded by pagan nations that practiced immoral rituals. So God needed to reestablish His covenant with His people.

Read **1 Corinthians 6:12-20**. As covenant partners with God, how should we treat our bodies?

Second, God circumcised the men…

To test their faith (Joshua 5:8)!

Look over **Joshua 5:8**. Based on this verse, what condition do you think the men of Israel were in?

Circumcision for adult men is usually very painful and will, no doubt, disable them for a little while. Since every military man was circumcised, we can believe that God's army was shut down for a bit. Imagine what could have happened if their enemies had attacked them during that time. God's people would have surely been slaughtered.

They just experienced victory when they crossed the Jordan River. Now, they are put in an extremely vulnerable position – a position where they needed to rely on God. Did you know that God often does this after victory? Great victories can lead to great pride. When pride is driving us, then we boast in ourselves, not in God. Nothing good ever comes from pride. God does His best and most powerful work when His people are depending solely on Him. I believe the people of God needed to learn this lesson as they rested and waited for healing.

What brought God's people victory, according to **2 Chronicles 13:18**?

Use **Hebrews 2:13** as your prayer right now.

Third, God circumcised the men...

To remove their reproach (Joshua 5:9)!

What name did God choose for the place they were staying **(Joshua 5:9)**?

The name *Gilgal* means "to roll." [1] In his commentary, *Be Strong*, Warren Wiersbe suggests that the "reproach of Egypt" refers to the ridicule of the enemy when Israel failed to trust God at Kadesh Barnea and enter the Promised Land.[2] In other words, Egypt must have mocked Israel when God failed to deliver them into their new land.

After the men healed from circumcision, the Israelites then celebrated **(Joshua 5:10-12)**. God renewed His covenant with them, gave them victory, removed their reproach, and was about to deliver them into a new land. They had every reason to celebrate.

How will you celebrate what God has done for you? Write out specific ways.

Day 2
The Commander's Appearance

The story of Israel conquering Jericho is not just an Old Testament narrative of a battle that took place thousands of years ago. It's a picture. A picture of *our* battles. We have stood in the very same place the Israelites are standing right now. We've glared at obstacles. Huge obstacles. Impossible situations. And we wonder. How in the world am I going to get through this? Can I fight this battle when I feel depleted already? Will I ever win?

Well, the historical event before us today gave Joshua the direction and assurance he needed as he prepared for the battle at Jericho. Before this encounter, he may have had just as many questions and doubts as we do. But right in the midst of his apprehension, God showed up. I mean, He actually showed up. And the encounter that takes place is for *our* benefit as much as it was for Joshua's. It surely caught Joshua off guard. In the end though, he was better prepared to lead God's people into their new awaited land.

As with any battle, we need to discover the best strategy that will work. Joshua is about to find out the correct and *only* strategy that will ensure a victory. We need to watch closely as God shows you and me how we can be victorious in our battles as well. A great unveiling today, I'm quite sure.

Read **Joshua 5:13-15** and describe the scene.

Where was Joshua **(Joshua 5:13)**?

As the people rested in Gilgal and the soldiers finished healing, Joshua takes a hike over to Jericho. I'm guessing that he was scoping out the territory because he knew they would be moving out soon, even though he did not know God's exact battle plan. As he was nearing Jericho, he encounters an unusual visitor.

What do you learn about this visitor **(verse 13)**? Be specific.

Scholars call this encounter a "theophany," which is a visible appearance of God. Because most theophanies in the Old Testament are actually visible appearances of Jesus, they are also called "christophanies." Either way, it seems that Joshua is looking into the face of Christ, who came in human form. That's the only way Joshua would have been able to look upon Him. Here's a great reminder: God always comes to us *when* we need Him and in the *way* we need Him.

Let's take a look at the way in which He showed up…

There are two significant things about this man we need to observe:

The man is…
1) standing
2) holding a drawn sword

With the heavy responsibility on Joshua's shoulders and the uncertainty of what is ahead, he looks up and sees a man. This is a sure sign that God is *with* Joshua. God is fulfilling what He told Joshua earlier: **"Do not be discouraged, for the LORD your God will be with you wherever you go" (Joshua 1:9)**. You and I can know that He is with us, too. Whether you're physically down, spiritually drained, emotionally spent, or just plain exhausted, He is *with* you. He doesn't just know what you need, but He comes to you in the midst of it. Our story today reminds us of this.

Ask God to reveal His presence to you right now in the midst of your struggle. Write down what He shows you.

A man standing with sword drawn is a military position. It shows that He's ready for combat. Imagine having this encounter. What was Joshua thinking? Were his eyes bulging? Hands trembling? Knees shaking? Was he scared? Confident? Awe-struck?

Why do you think God came to Joshua like this? And at this moment?

Upon seeing this man, Joshua was confused. He asked a logical question: "Are you for us or for our enemies?"

How did the man respond **(verse 14)**?

One commentator said that perhaps He was saying, "I'm not here to take sides, but to take over."[3] This seems sensible when you read the remaining part of the text. But how Joshua responds shows why he was one of heaven's greatest leaders, warriors. Let's take a look…

Joshua responded…

In humility!

Joshua finally recognized this man as divinely sent. And he responded exactly the way he should have. Our text says that he **"fell facedown to the ground" (Joshua 5:14)**.

What did God say to Jehoshaphat just before they were attacked in **2 Chronicles 20:15**?

We often think that God has come to fight *our* battles. But God reminds Jehoshaphat that the battle is not his, nor is it the Israelites' battle. It's GOD'S battle. So, whatever battle you are in with the enemy, it's not your battle. Your job, as Joshua demonstrates, is to be a *soldier* and a *servant* at the same time.

In his commentary on Joshua, Warren Wiersbe quotes the great Chinese Bible teacher, Watchman Nee: "Not until we take the place of a servant can He take His place as Lord."[4] Wow! That changes my perspective. Does it change yours?

Joshua responded…

In worship!

Our text says that Joshua **"fell facedown to the ground in *reverence*" (Joshua 5:14)**.

Reverence is a position one takes in honoring God for who He is. Joshua was putting God in His rightful place, while taking a lower position.

Worship should always precede movement. Worship opens the door for God to work. Worship causes our God to get bigger. And worship put Joshua and God's people in the perfect position for victory.

Joshua responded…

In submission!

After Joshua fell and worshiped, he then submitted to God's plan by asking, **"What message does my Lord have for his servant" (Joshua 5:14)**?

This title reveals what position God was to take in the battle: the *commander of the LORD's Army*.

What instruction did the commander of the LORD's army give to Joshua in **Joshua 5:15**?

How did Joshua respond?

Joshua displays one of the most important aspects to a great leader: letting go of his own purpose and submitting to God's purposes. But here's a sad reality: this feature often eludes Christian leaders.

Below are three ways leaders lead. Circle which one should be the correct way based on our story:

1) Make our plans and carry them out to the best of our ability!
2) Lay our plans out and ask God to help us!
3) Begin with God. Ask Him for His plans and then offer ourselves to Him.

No doubt, you circled # 3. When we begin with God and offer ourselves to Him, we lead people *to* Christ. It is then that God pours out His blessings. And here's the best part: submitting to God's ways always leads to victory. The world balks at this kind of leadership and often mocks those who lead this way. But remember that we aren't working for the world; we are working for God. Joshua has surely shown us how to be a great warrior, leader, and soldier.

So, let's throw down our weapons and submit to Him now as our rightful King.

Our story concludes with Joshua's response to the commander's request. Joshua took off his sandals. Removing ones sandals was a sign of *servanthood*, *respect* and *submission*.

In the end, Joshua went out to battle the enemy in the power of the Lord. I say "Amen!"

Take a moment to review today's lesson. What one truth stands out the most to you? Why?

Day 3
God's Battle Plan

In her book, *I Saw the Lord*, Anne Graham Lotz writes: "Those of us who call ourselves by God's name need a fresh vision of the greatness of Jesus Christ."[5] There's nothing more truthful than this. The prophet Isaiah's mission was tough. He was to tell a calloused people to repent. None of us would want that job. God, however, prepared him by letting him catch a vision of Jesus sitting on His throne **(Isaiah 6:1-4)**. I'm thinking that Isaiah was never quite the same. Peter had a similar encounter with Jesus **(Luke 5:1-11)** when he recognized Christ's divinity next to his own humanity. No doubt, this changed Peter's perspective and prepared him for his future work as leader of the early church. And then on a remote island, John – an old man by then – saw Jesus **(Revelation 1:9-18)** shining in marvelous brilliance. John was given a peak into future prophesies. Imagine living the rest of your days with *this* vision seared into your mind.

Like many before him, Joshua was called for a difficult job. It wasn't easy to transition from member of a nation to leader. Moses had set a good precedent by obeying God fully and laying down guidelines for the people. In reality, though, nothing could have prepared Joshua for what was ahead. That is until God showed up and Joshua encountered Christ in the flesh **(Joshua 5:13-15)**. He witnessed the power and authority of God before his very eyes. A fresh vision! Now, Joshua's heart has been set ablaze and he's ready to move forward to conquer the land.

What are you up against right now? Are you tired of running? Perhaps you need a fresh vision of Jesus. Before you go any further in your study today, open up Scripture and ask God to awaken your eyes to see Jesus like you've never seen Him before. Record your vision.

Read **Joshua 6:1-21**. Write out God's battle plan.

Let's begin today's lesson with a crucial piece of information. What did God tell Joshua in **Joshua 6:2**?

God's word here to Joshua sets the stage for a powerful conclusion to this battle. God tells Joshua pragmatically that the land was *already* theirs. God had already claimed it for His people. Do you see how this news changes everything? Victory was theirs. He's just reiterating what He had already told Moses decades earlier: **"I have come down to rescue them from the hand of the Egyptians and to bring them out of that land into a good and spacious land, a land flowing with milk and honey" (Exodus 3:8)**.

So then, why didn't the people take possession of the land years before? Why now, four decades later? Well, it has to do with how the people responded. Remember, this is a new generation and they have different attitudes. The first group to exit Egypt didn't believe God and they often struggled to obey Moses. They grumbled, complained, and doubted that God could deliver them into the land **(Numbers 14:1-4)**. Therefore, their postponed entrance into the Promised Land had to do with *unbelief* and *disobedience*.

Did you know that we've been offered a promised land as well? Describe it based on **John 10:10**?

This is *our* land flowing with milk and honey.

Look up the following verses and write down what this full life includes.

John 14:27:

Galatians 5:1:

Matthew 11:28:

1 Corinthians 15:57:

Colossians 1:27:

Galatians 5:22-23:

Here's the thing: Jesus paid the "full life" price for you and me. He signed the papers with His blood. Done deal! But let me go out on a limb and suggest that many believers are not experiencing the rich life Jesus came to give them. Why not? Well, like the Israelites, it has to do with unbelief and disobedience. So here are a few questions we can ask ourselves that might help us in our quest for abundant living.

Are you trusting Him in your circumstances, or are you complaining and worrying?
Do you believe what He has said, or do you doubt?
Are you obeying His precepts, or are you simply doing what you want?
Have you said "yes" to God, even if you don't understand God's ways?
Are you holding tight to His promises, or are you neglecting His Word?

Based on the above questions, write down what might be keeping you from the abundant life. Then write out your prayer asking God to help you claim what He's offering you.

Now, let's continue with our story in Joshua.

Read again **Joshua 6:3-4**? What is the common number?

What are the exact instructions listed in these verses?

In biblical numerology, the #7 represents completeness or perfection. The word *seven* comes from the Hebrew word *shevah* and means, "to be full, to be satisfied." [6] The #7 is a sacred number to God's people and can be traced all the way back to Genesis when God created the world in six days and rested on the seventh day. Hence, it was done, finished! Completed! Perhaps He chose seven days of marching and seven priests carrying trumpets to signify that His prophesy was being fulfilled and would be complete.

Would you say that God's battle plan is highly unusual? There was no training in combat, instruction in weapons, defense exercises, or attack techniques. It made no sense. Here are two things we can gain from this scene. Think of each one in relation to your own battles.

The Israelites had to…

1. Believe God!

Joshua was God's spokesperson, so the people had to trust that he had heard from God. They surely needed confidence that this was God's plan, even though it made no sense to them. They must believe that He would do what He said He would do.

No battle had ever been fought this way before. What was God up to? Did they understand? No. The only thing they could do was put their concerns aside and walk on faith. The writer of Hebrews says, **"Without faith it is impossible to please God" (Hebrews 11:6)**. Faith is one feature that God looks for in His people. He honors those who walk in faith, even if they can't see what's ahead.

Compare **Hebrews 11:1** with our story in Joshua.

How did the people exemplify belief, and how did God honor it?

The Israelites had to…

2. Walk in obedience!

March around the city once for six days, and then seven times on the seventh day? Really? And no talking? You've got to be kidding! Have you ever mumbled something similar to yourself when God asked you to do something that seemed absurd?

Throughout Scripture God blesses those who obey. As I write this, I think about how writing is not something I thought I would ever do. My brain doesn't like to think sometimes. That's why I slid through high school by the skin of my teeth. In Bible College I did much better, but I still didn't like to study much. And writing Bible studies requires lots of reading and research. But I know God has called me to it. In fact, if my writing touches one person's heart by opening Scripture to them, then it's absolutely worth it. *God surely blesses obedience*.

Before we conclude with today's lesson, let me give you some food for thought:

- The trumpets were *rams horns* (shofar). These trumpets were primarily for celebrations. We should celebrate what God has done for us, too.
- The priests were to keep their eyes on the Ark of the Covenant (God's presence). We are told to keep our eyes on things above, not on things of the earth **(Colossians 3:2)**.
- God had already claimed the victory for Israel. He's done the same for us **(1 Corinthians 15:57)**, so we can – and should – live like victors, not victims.

Review today's lesson and write down what you heard God say to you. How will you put these truths into practice in the midst of your circumstances?

Day 4
Redemptive Purposes

I heard a speaker once say that we should *never* put a lid on our spiritual box. This made me think of how I've done just that. I grew up in a traditional church, with conservative views. While I'm proud of my heritage and the biblical foundation I received in my growing-up years, I realized that I had gathered my beliefs, stuffed them into a box, and crammed a lid on top. Then I tucked it safely under my bed. Hence, there was no wiggle room to experience more. I was satisfied with what I knew about God, His ways, and His purposes.

But then I heard those words from that speaker. As I did some soul-searching, I came to the conclusion that it was wrong to close up my box. Why? Because God is really BIG. In fact, He's much BIGGER than my little theological box. When God revealed that to me, I crouched under my bed, slid out the make-believe box, and removed the lid. God has more to teach me, I'm sure of it. But of course, I still test everything through Scripture – since there's so much false theology permeating the church today – before endorsing it.

God's redemptive purposes trace all the way back to the book of Genesis. As we pour over Scripture, we find that God often goes to the utmost places to bring people salvation. He scours the countryside and invites anyone in – anyone who will believe. It doesn't matter where they've come from, what despicable things they've done, or what culture they've been immersed in. And often these people, who have been redeemed by God's grace, have been used mightily for God's purposes.

Today we come upon one person who was blessed to be a part of God's redemptive purposes. Our journey takes us back to a woman we came to know earlier – a woman we called an unlikely heroine of the Old Testament: *Rahab*.

We will disclose four marvelous things about Rahab. But before we jump in, we need to review what we learned about Rahab already. Please go back to Week 2 and look through Day 5. What three things did we regard about Rahab?

1. _____
2. _____
3. _____

Based on these things, why do you think Rahab made a splash in biblical history?

Now stay with me because our lesson will unveil extraordinary hope as we watch God's redemptive purposes unfold. Let's look at four ways in which Rahab has become an integral part of God's redemptive purposes.

1. Rahab's favor!

Summarize **Joshua 6:22-25**.

What do you understand about God in this passage?

What benefit(s) was Rahab awarded?

This is God's favor being poured out. Truly impressive, don't you agree? It's important to note that this isn't the end of Rahab's story. It's just the beginning.

Who is your God, according to **Deuteronomy 7:9**?

Do you believe God's favor can be poured out on us, today? Let **Proverbs 8:34-35** answer this question.

According to these verses, how can we receive favor from the Lord?

I started feeding hummingbirds this year. They are interesting creatures and so fun to watch, especially as they make their territorial claims. As I write this, I see a little guy sitting on a limb outside my window protecting the bird feeder. He chases away other birds if they try to invade his territory. I learned that the hummingbird metabolism goes so fast that they are always on a hunt to find food. Food is their highest priority since their little bellies are forever hungry.

Let me tell you what I want more than anything. I want to have such a ravenous hunger for spiritual food, that I am always on a hunt for more spiritual food. You've heard the old adage: "Be the kind of woman that when your feet hit the floor in the morning, the devil says, 'Oh darn, she's up!'" You may have noticed that I changed one word in the phrase so as not to offend anyone, but it still has the same meaning. If the devil actually said that, it would be awesome because then it would mean that God's favor is all over me.

Let's use **Psalm 90:17** as our prayer:

"May the favor of the Lord [my] God rest upon [me]; establish the work of [my hands] – yes, establish the work of [my] hands."

2. Rahab's legacy!

As we get older, we think about what kind of legacy we want to leave behind after we're gone. Someone recently told me that she is working tirelessly on photo books she hopes to leave for her grandchildren. A worthy gift, no doubt. In Rahab's day, there was no such thing as cameras. However, I believe her legacy is far more worthy than pictures anyway.

Look up the following verses and write down what legacy Rahab left:

Hebrews 11:31:

James 2:25:

In both cases, the New Testament writers wrote about Rahab's faith. It was her faith that brought down God's favor upon her. Rahab's name is listed in the *"Hall of Faith Museum"* **(Hebrews 11)** alongside many other great faith heroes. What an honor! And then James mentions her in his dialogue on how to live by faith.

We don't have a photograph of Rahab – and we can only vaguely understand her story – but in the end, she has made indelible impressions upon the Church. A lasting legacy.

Does this spur something inside of you? What?

What legacy do you want to leave behind? Are you living now the way you should in order to leave that legacy? Write down your thoughts.

3. Rahab's lineage!

This one is so cool. There are a couple genealogies listed in the New Testament **(Matthew 1:1-16; Luke 3:23-38)**, but most of us have never taken the time to study them. Today, however, we will look closely at Matthew's account. Matthew traces Abraham's line all the way to Jesus – this is the line that David and Jesus came from.

Skim over the list **(Matthew 1:1-16)**.

Now, focus on **verse 5**. Do you see a familiar name? Who?

That's right! Rahab the former prostitute is listed in Jesus' genealogy. It's surely not an accident that Rahab (a woman) is mentioned in this list. Since it is comprised of mostly men, I'm sure God wanted us to know that Rahab was an integral part of God's redemptive purposes.

In what ways does Rahab represent you and me?

Look up the following verses. What has God done for you?

Psalm 40:2-3:

Ephesians 2:4-10:

Here's something you and I need to chew on for a while: Like Rahab, we, too, are an *integral* part of God's redemptive purposes.

What do you say about that? What words will us use to describe God's awesome work in your life?

4. Rahab's inheritance!

When Rahab was rescued from her collapsed city, what happened to her **(Joshua 6:25)**?

Rahab went from pauper to princess, basically. She was brought into a new family and given all the rights, privileges, and rewards the Israelites were awarded in their new land. But the best inheritance she received for her faith was a life of eternity in heaven with God. Something tells me that she felt wealthy beyond anything she had ever dreamed of.

You and I have been given a GREAT inheritance as well. Look up **1 Peter 1:3-5** and write down what it is.

I've read this passage a thousand times and it still gives me chills. We are rich beyond measure and because we believed and said *yes* to God, like Rahab, we are awarded great treasures in heaven. Paul tells us that **"Jesus Christ has blessed us in the heavenly realms with *every* spiritual blessing in Christ" (Ephesians 1:3)**. Not just some spiritual blessings, but all of them. If that doesn't get you excited, I don't know what will.

Please take a moment and review today's lesson. What stands out to you about Rahab and how would you like to emulate her life?

Day 5
A Fatal Mistake

I have been in ministry almost my entire adult life and here's what I've seen to be true: Satan *always* shows up when God is on the move. Satan hates God and hates His people, especially the most loyal ones. Therefore, he will do whatever he can to thwart God's plans by causing chaos, division, and turmoil. Today I was driving home from the gym and praying for a person who has been causing me grief. And then I remembered that I'm about to begin a Bible study. Now it makes sense: Satan wants me so flustered with feelings of inadequacy and frustration that I'll give up. Well, he should realize by now that his little antics only push me harder *toward* God, not running in the opposite direction.

We have watched God work in mighty ways to conquer the land that rightfully belonged to His people. We witnessed miracle after miracle. The walls of Jericho fell into a heap on the ground as God delivered His beloved people into their awaited land. No more living in the desert. No doubt, the people are high on joy right about now. Let the celebrations begin!

But as the people reveled in excitement, they were unaware of what was lurking in the shadows. Their greatest enemy was waiting for the right moment to make his move. He was looking for the perfect opportunity – like a cat inching toward its prey just waiting to pounce. And as always, it didn't take Satan long to find it. Joy would turn to sorrow. Excitement would convert to discouragement. And harmony would give way to pandemonium.

Satan would use one man to do his bidding: *Achan*. This is a story we should ponder hard because it's a picture of what happens when sin reins – then and *now*.

Before we begin today's reading, let's back up to a vital piece of information Joshua spoke before the people. In a few words, what did he say about the Canaanite stuff in the city **(Joshua 6:17-18)**?

Now, read **Joshua 7:1-26**. Briefly describe what has just happened.

Have you ever made a mistake that cost you big? Maybe where someone else, besides you, got hurt in the process? Or perhaps your mistake resulted in you losing someone or something you cherished? Here are a few examples:

- A teenager sends an improper photo to a friend's phone and it gets shared on social media. She loses her integrity.
- A woman says some nasty things to a friend in the heat of emotion. She loses a great friendship.
- A school basketball star cheats on an exam. He loses his place on the team and a coveted scholarship.

- A pastor engages in an improper relationship. He loses his position and his respect.
- A writer plagiarizes someone else's work. She loses her publishing contract and her esteem.

I just read of a young college-aged couple who thought it would be fun to jump a train. In the middle of the night, when the train was going through town at 4-5 miles per hour, they both fell off. She died and her boyfriend was injured. What a tragic mistake that cost them immensely.

I don't think Achan left home that day vowing to steal something. It just happened – a mistake. But a sin, nonetheless. God had made everything sacred and he violated God's covenant.

After he was found out and confronted, how did he respond? **(Joshua 7:20-21)**?

I'm not sure Achan had a true repentant heart, though. If he had, wouldn't he have confessed before being found out? Just thinking. But in case you're wondering, we just learned the sequence to sin: Achan said, I *saw*… I *coveted*… I *took*.

Coveting is the itch for more money, property, possessions, success, esteem, status, fame, popularity, position, and personal appearance. The Babylonian robe Achan *saw*, *coveted*, and then *took* was a status symbol. Josephus, the Jewish historian, says that this garment was a royal robe woven entirely of gold.[7]

Write out James' full description of the sequence of sin (**James 1:14-15**).

I could write a whole Bible study on **Joshua 7** alone. But for the sake of time, let's hone in on the results of sin based on this story, and then conclude with a glorious principle. Here's what we learn from Achan's mistake:

Sin results in defeat!

Explain this consequence for the nation of Israel in **Joshua 7:1-5**.

Let me remind you that up until now in the book of Joshua, the Israelites experienced triumphant victory. Now they're facing defeat. In addition to the sin issue, I see something else at work in this narrative that is sure to have contributed to their defeat: *overconfidence* and *pride*. The people had just conquered Jericho, and now they're on to the next city, Ai (pronounced like the letter "I"). It seems to me that when Joshua sent men to spy out Ai, they looked around and thought, "Oh that's easy. This city is small in comparison to Jericho." So they reported to Joshua that only two or three thousand men would be required to overtake this place, unlike the approximate 40,000 soldiers who marched around Jericho.[8]

Why do you think overconfidence and pride could have contributed to their defeat?

What insight does **Proverbs 16:18** shed on pride?

When we become overconfident or prideful, we lean the wrong way. Instead of leaning on God, we lean on *ourselves*. Instead of trusting in God to help us, we trust in *our* abilities. We can never experience victory in Christ by ourselves. Never!

In spite of the overconfidence and pride issue, Achan's sin was the biggest culprit here. Oh, the ugliness of sin. The nation of Israel should have easily conquered Ai. Instead, they ran home fearing for their lives, and leaving behind some of their comrades dead on the battlefield.

Are you feeling defeated in some area of your life? Could it be the way you are leaning? Or could it be some unconfessed sin you haven't dealt with? Perhaps right now is a good time for some soul-searching. What has God shown you?

Sin affects every area of our lives!

Read the following portions of Scripture from our text and write what happened.

Joshua 7:4-5:

Joshua 7:12:

Joshua 7:24-25:

Because of one impulsive move and taking what didn't belong to him, Achan lost everything. He lost his respect, his family, his possessions, his favor with God, and ultimately, his life. In fact, the whole nation suffered. Thirty-six innocent men lost their lives that day. Sin has grave consequences.

What words of wisdom does God offer in **Jeremiah 23:24**?

What does sin do to us, according to **Proverbs 5:22**?

Sin enslaves us. But the consequences of sin go far beyond the one who sins. Everyone and everything is affected: our relationships, our marriages, our work, and our ministries. It robs us of peace, joy, hope, and the fruit of the Spirit. In addition to all of these things, sin hinders our fellowship with Christ and keeps us from hearing the voice of God.

This morning a radio host was talking about how marriage partners often want to give up on their marriage when things become difficult. They choose to walk out of one marriage for another one. He said that what they don't realize is that second marriages have a higher divorce rate than first marriages. He concluded with this: rather than run to another marriage, we need to try and fix the one we're in. Of course, many have tried to no avail. God surely doesn't hold you accountable if you've tried.

This brings us to our last point...

Sin needs to be addressed!

Skim over **Joshua 7:10-13**. What did God tell Joshua?

What did Joshua do **(Joshua 7:19, 22-25)**?

Confronting sin is always hard, especially when you're a leader. But Joshua needs to set the example and obey God. Addressing our own sin is hard, too. But when we repent and turn away from it, we are set free from its mastery over us. Sometimes the consequences linger, but our spirits are set free. And then we revel in victory, not fall in defeat. The nation of Israel could now move forward with Joshua leading and God directing the way. Why? Because sin had been addressed and dealt with.

We *will* sin because we're human and we have a fleshly nature. But it's important that we keep our eyes on Scripture so that we will know when sin has taken root in our hearts.

After we address sin and confess it **(1 John 1:9)**, what promise can we cling to, according to **Hebrews 10:17**?

Joshua is showing us what true leadership is. He's demonstrating how to be the kind of warrior God needs on His team. What are you learning from Joshua?

Ponder our lesson today. Do you see yourself in Achan's story? Joshua's position? Is God revealing something to you that you need to address? Write out your thoughts.

I hope you're witnessing great truths presented in the book of Joshua. We have two weeks to go. Don't give up. It will all come together like a beautiful masterpiece. Thank you for taking this journey with me.

1. LOGOS: Warren Wiersbe, *Be Strong*.
2. LOGOS: Warren Wiersbe, *Be Strong*.
3. https://bible.org/article/captain-lord%E2%80%99s-army-joshua-513-15
4. LOGOS: Warren Wiersbe, *Be Strong*.
5. Anne Graham Lotz, *I Saw The Lord* (Grand Rapids, MI, Zondervan, 2006), 87.
6. LOGOS: Warren Wiersbe, *Be Strong*.
7. https://banneroftruth.org/us/resources/articles/2007/the-sin-of-achan/
8. http://www.bibletrack.org/notes/resource/misc/Jericho.html

Week 5
Marching Fearlessly

Day 1
Brilliant Strategy
Day 2
Deceived and Defrauded
Day 3
Audacious Faith
Day 4
Conquering the Land
Day 5
Fighting Offensively

Do you remember the words God said to Joshua at the beginning of his reign? He said, **"Be strong and courageous. Do not be terrified; do not be discouraged, for the LORD your God will be with you wherever you go" (Joshua 1:9).** Something tells me that these words slipped Joshua's mind periodically (as they do ours), because God spoke the same words to him just before the attack on Ai: **"The Lord said to Joshua, 'Do not be afraid; do not be discouraged'" (Joshua 8:1).** I'm fairly certain that it wasn't a memory lapse that caused him to forget, but probably overwhelming circumstances. Or maybe he just needed to hear them again. No matter, some truths need repeating. This is surely one of those truths.

For forty years after the exodus from Egypt, Moses led the people of God. After he died, God raised up Joshua to lead. Two leaders. Two completely different administrations. Moses brought the Law, erected the Tabernacle, and met with God in the Tent of Meeting. He wore many different hats as leader, counselor, preacher, and judge. In the desert, the Israelites became a nation. Moses introduced the people to God.

Joshua, on the other hand, was trained and prepared not just to be a leader, but to be a *military* leader. His direction would take a divergent path than Moses. Moses led a flock in the wilderness. Joshua would lead an army into combat. But as Joshua walked before the people with the Law in his hands, God said, **"Do not let this Book of the Law depart from your mouth; meditate on it day and night, so that you may be careful to do everything written in it" (Joshua 1:8).**

We will soon find out that Joshua lived by God's word because the soldiers marched forth to conquer the land *fearlessly*. Trust and obedience led the people forward to claim what was rightfully theirs. And God never left their side. This week we will learn how we, too, can live fearlessly. Let's follow Joshua into the land of promise – the land already occupied.

Day 1
Brilliant Strategy

How did God explain the land of Israel to Moses **(Exodus 3:17)**?

Look up **Deuteronomy 8:7-9** and write a description of this land.

If you had wandered like nomads in the desert your entire life and buried most of your family in that place, wouldn't you be excited to *finally* get a new land – a land as picture perfect as what Moses described? Wouldn't you be chomping at the bit to get there? The other day I was talking to someone about how it feels to be getting older. He told me that it's strange because while he knows that the life awaiting him is so much better, he's not ready to leave *this* life. I understand what he's saying, but I feel like the older I get, the more excited I am to get to my eternal home – a place far better than what I've ever known. Something tells me that a majority of those who crossed the Jordan River felt that way, too.

But unlike the entrance into *our* new land, the Israelites' entrance wasn't quite as easy. I heard it said that the Promised Land was actually a *problem land*. The land God described to Moses – a land "flowing with milk and honey" – was occupied by wicked and idolatrous people. Nations of people not easily defeated.

According to **Deuteronomy 7:1**, what do you learn about these nations?

Sometimes we have to go through the bad in order to get to the good. Don't you find that it often gets worse before it gets better? So therefore, it's important we don't give up. Keep God's Word before you and His promises tucked safely in your heart, bringing them out often. God is *always* faithful. ALWAYS!

What piece of information did God give to His people about conquering the land **(Deuteronomy 7:22)**?

The land was taken in stages and Joshua used a brilliant strategy called *divide and conquer*. In fact, this military strategy has been used throughout history in many battles. We witnessed Joshua and his army conquer the first major city, Jericho. Today we come to the second city, Ai. These two cities, Jericho and Ai, were centrally located in Israel. After they were conquered, Joshua moved toward the southern cities, and then marched up to the north. If he had started in the south first, the central and northern cities would have joined together and become a stronger foe. Joshua is certainly a great military leader.

Let's pause here for a moment and ponder this divide and conquer method. It's truly a smart battle plan when conquering land. However, it's *never* a good method in places where unity is of utmost importance. You've heard it said, *united we stand, divided we fall*. Well, that's very true because unity harvests strength, but division yields weakness.

Read Jesus' words in **Matthew 12:25**. What warning does He give?

This is a warning we need to heed, yet we often don't. Look around and you'll see the divide and conquer approach at work in families, the church, the country, and the world. Children prevail at pitting their parents against each other. Christians succeed at dividing the church right down the middle. Co-workers stand on opposite sides of the room throwing accusations in each other's faces. Nations gang up on other nations. And people let their disagreements tear friendships apart.

Here's the thing: when we are divided, then Satan conquers our hearts, our minds, our emotions, our peace, and our joy. He is an expert at destroying what was once really good.

In what ways have you seen division around you?

Perhaps it's time to ask God to bridge the divide. And then *do* everything you can to close up the gap. How will you do this?

Okay, we must move on. Today we come to the second city to be conquered: Ai. Read **Joshua 8:1-29**. What approach did Joshua and the Israelites take in conquering this city?

Why do you imagine God would use this method to overtake the city?

Why do you think we are sometimes like the people of Ai?

When natural disasters threaten certain areas, sometimes the governor of a state will issue mandatory evacuations. In other words, there is a real threat headed your way and you had better get out. Last year, a major hurricane was about to make a direct hit on a family member's city. A mandatory evacuation was called and just about everyone in her town fled, except she and her husband. After it was over, they had minimal damage and no injuries, but it could have been much worse. She promised her family they will never do that again.

The people of Ai had heard about the God of the Israelites. They must have heard about the destruction in Jericho and that no one, except a woman and her family, survived. And they must have been aware that Joshua, the leader of the people, was a master strategist. Imagine the fear that gripped the townspeople when they realized that Ai was next on the Israelites' hit list. So why wouldn't they take every precaution to protect their people and their city?

What exactly happened, according to **Joshua 8:16-17**?

The attack on Ai reveals two sides: the awful side of *defeat* and the glorious side of *victory*. Let's look closer at both sides.

The awful side of defeat!

Why do you think the people of Ai were so easily defeated?

The bait had been set and the people of Ai were *lured* away, leaving their city and the occupants completely vulnerable to attack. Every man fled the city. The trap worked. The men of Israel who had set the ambush rushed in and took the city, destroying everything. And then they joined forces to destroy the men who had left the city.

We will discuss more about Satan in tomorrow's lesson, but I will say that he's got patience. He waits until we let our guard down and then when we're not paying attention, he swoops in for the kill. He uses this tactic frequently. When we let our guard down, we put ourselves in a vulnerable spot, like sitting ducks. When we let our guard down, we *will* be defeated.

Let me ask you, have you let your guard down? Have you become complacent, unconcerned that the roaring lion is seeking for someone to devour **(1 Peter 5:8)**?

How are we instructed to live, according to **Ephesians 6:10-18**?

The glorious side of victory!

Why do you think the Israelite army was victorious in capturing the city of Ai?

Joshua instructed the people what to do and they did it. They didn't let fear keep them back. Perhaps they learned a hard lesson from their ancestors when fear gripped the entire population **(Numbers 13:31-14:4)**. Victory is so much better than defeat.

What keeps us from being victorious in our lives?

Sometimes we let fear stop us. Other times, we let people's doubts or negativity sway us. Or sometimes we just don't believe our God is BIG enough. But we can learn a lot from the Israelites in this story. They listened to their leader and did what he commanded. No complaining. No arguing. They positioned themselves exactly where Joshua told them to. They moved forward fearlessly. Oh, the glorious side of victory. How wonderful it is.

What is God speaking to you about right now?

Let's conclude today's lesson with one final picture. Read **Joshua 8:30:35** and summarize what they did after conquering the city.

Sometimes we forget to give glory to God in the moment of victory. I believe that showing our gratitude and offering true sacrifices are more important than the victory itself.

How will you honor God today for what He's done for you?

Day 2
Deceived and Defrauded

I know people who are easily swayed by the sweet talker, the charmer, the manipulator. They know exactly what to say to get the person they're trying to dupe to give them what they want. These people are dishonest and deceitful. Some people are so trusting that they'll believe anything they say. Cheaters are not just in movies, but they are living among us. They're in the church. They use people's weaknesses to gain control. Now listen to me carefully: Christians can easily get victimized just because someone mentions God. I know a group of Christians who lost their life savings because they trusted in a fellow church member's investment. He took their money and ran.

You would think that Joshua would not be so easily fooled. But right in the beginning of conquering the land, he was tricked. In fact, we can see Satan all over this story, so it's vital we pay attention. Today we come to a scene that will leave us shaking our heads. Sometimes I'm skeptical of certain people, but I also have a trusting spirit. Whether you are skeptical or trusting, the lesson before us today is for everyone. You and I need to learn how to protect ourselves from being deceived and defrauded.

Read **Joshua 9:1-27** and answer the following questions.

Who were the Gibeonites and what did they do?

How did Joshua and the leaders respond in this situation?

Before we move forward with our study, we need to go back to earlier instructions God gave to the people. What were the instructions, according to **Exodus 34:12** and **Deuteronomy 20:16-17**?

Why were they commanded to destroy the entire city when conquering the whole land **(Deuteronomy 20:18)**?

The Gibeonites must have known this mandate, so they resorted to trickery to save their own necks. Gibeon was only twenty-five miles from Gilgal, but they disguised themselves and pretended they were from far away. As the Gibeonites presented themselves to Joshua and the leaders of Israel, we see two opposing sides: the evil (Satan) side, and the good (the representatives of God) side. This story surely reveals how easy it is for the representatives of God to be deceived. There are three crucial things we learn about Satan in this story:

Satan masquerades as an angel of light (2 Corinthians 11:14)!

How do you see this working in the men of Gibeon **(Joshua 9:3-5)**?

Why do you think this characteristic of Satan is so dangerous? How have you witnessed this?

I believe there are *many* people in our churches in disguises. Joshua and the leaders didn't recognize the façade of the Gibeonites because these deceivers took great measures to put on old tattered clothes and carry worn-out wineskins. They looked authentic – like they were who they claimed to be. Warren Wiersbe said, "It's much easier for us to identify the lion when he's roaring than to detect the serpent when he's slithering into our lives." [1]

What is one clue that can help us pick these people out **(2 Timothy 3:5)**?

Ask them questions and find out what they believe about God. The one masquerading will skirt around the issue and eventually deny the power of God. We need to be very careful when we put our faith in people because way too many innocent souls have been scammed.

Satan lies (John 8:44)!

According to **Joshua 9:6**, how do you see this principle at work in the Gibeonites?

Satan isn't just a liar, but he's the father of lies **(John 8:44)**. The Gibeonites looked Joshua right in the eyes and lied to him. You and I know what that feels like. We feel violated, taken advantage of. The church is full of hypocrites and they're getting more and more prevalent the closer we get to Jesus' return.

Satan deceives!

What is Jesus warning in **Matthew 24:4-5?**

In light of this, how did the Gibeonites deceive the leaders of Israel **(Joshua 9:9-10)**?

Christians can easily get fooled by imposters. Some of them just say the name of God. This is one of Satan's favorite tactics to get to us. Remember that he boldly quoted Scripture to Jesus in the desert **(Matthew 4:1-11)**. Again, we need to test what people say. We need to compare their words to Scripture.

Look over the three things about Satan evident in this story. In what ways have you seen him use these ploys in your life, your family, your ministry, your church, your community, or your relationships?

Hang tight. I promise we will gain some practical remedies to deal with Satan's attacks.

Answer the following questions:

What did Joshua and the leaders *not* do **(Joshua 9:14)**?

What did Joshua and the leaders *do* **(Joshua 9:15)**?

We may ask, "Why did Joshua and the leaders not recognize their deception? Why did they sign a treaty with them, when they were clearly warned not to **(Exodus 34:12)**? The answer is right in this verse, **"They did not inquire of the Lord" (Joshua 9:14)**. Instead, they used human reasoning by examining the facts, discussing the matter, and agreeing together to a conclusion. These things are never bad, but used alone, can be costly. If they had sought the Lord's counsel before making a treaty with them, God would have revealed the evil intentions of the Gibeonites. Pastor Skip Heitzig says, "Divine proximity to the Lord is how to wise up to Satan's attacks."

Compare **John 7:17** to our passage in **Joshua 9**. What is Jesus' wise counsel?

What does James tell us **(James 1:5)**?

Are you in the process of making an agreement with someone? A business partnership? A marriage proposal? A church assignment? Or some other joint venture? If so, write down what it is and what you'll do before you ever sign your name on the dotted line.

Let's conclude with one more important detail. When Joshua and the leaders found out they had been tricked, what did they do according to **Joshua 9:18-22**?

This is interesting. They couldn't go back on their word, so they made it work for them. They did not allow them to continue as a free nation. Instead, they brought them in as woodcutters and water carriers. Hence, the Gibeonites were in close contact with the Israelites and their God. Rather than worshiping their false deities, they sat among the Jewish people and heard about the One true God. We find out later that the men of Gibeon helped, alongside Nehemiah, in rebuilding the walls of Jerusalem **(Nehemiah 3:7)**. It seems that the mistake Joshua and the leaders made turned out for good. God used it mightily.

What have you gained from today's lesson? What truth will you take with you today?

Day 3
Audacious Faith

I can think of several defining moments in my life. Of course, the moment I received Jesus as my Savior was certainly a defining moment. And the day God spoke to my heart and instructed me to apply to Bible College. One other time resonates in my mind: the moment the Holy Spirit gave me complete and miraculous peace when I, on the verge of having a panic attack, stood before the congregation at church to speak. A defining moment is a point at which the essential nature or character of a person is revealed or defined. All of these defining moments in my life unveiled the deep faith in my spirit.

Can you think of a defining moment in your life? What did you learn about yourself?

The story we are about to study today is surely a defining moment in Joshua's life as leader of the Israelites. An amazing miracle they witnessed with their own eyes. And, no doubt, the people of Israel recounted – years later – the day their fearless leader boldly prayed, in the midst of battle, for the sun to stand still. In today's narrative, we will see a characteristic about Joshua that will truly inspire us in our walk with Christ: an *audacious faith*.

Slowly read **Joshua 10:1-15** taking it all in. In your own words, summarize this story.

Obviously we could spend a great deal of time on this miracle, but for the sake of time we will cover the most important aspects in this passage.

According to **Joshua 10:1-5**, how many kings were there and what did they plan to do? Why?

Hatred, betrayal, desperation, and feeling threatened drive people to do all sorts of not-so-good things. I sense you agreeing with me because you've seen it with your own eyes. In this case, it seems that the king of Jerusalem felt betrayed by the Gibeonites, and also threatened by the Israelite army. The footnote in my NIV study Bible referencing this passage states: "Perhaps he [the king of Jerusalem] held [or claimed] some political dominion over the Gibeonite cities and viewed their submission to Israel as rebellion." [2] So in desperation, he appealed to the other kings and formed a coalition against the Gibeonites.

When the joined army came to declare war, what did the Gibeonites do **(Joshua 10:6)**?

Based on **Joshua 9:15**, why did the Gibeonites appeal to Joshua?

A good reputation always precedes an exemplary leader. The Israelites' reputation went before them and all the surrounding nations knew this, especially the Gibeonites. Joshua made a promise and he intended to keep it. So the Gibeonites relied on his word. What a good lesson for us. God is One who *never* goes back on His word. He is a covenant-keeping, promise-keeping God.

What promise do you need to lean into today? Is it strength **(Philippians 4:13)**? Wisdom **(James 1:5)**? Protection **(John 17:12)**? Patience **(Galatians 5:22)**? Deliverance **(Psalm 3:8)**? Hope **(Hebrews 6:19)**?

Or is it some other promise? Take a moment to examine what's going on in your life right now and choose a biblical promise you need to cling to. Write down the verse and recite it as many time as you need to, until it takes up residence in your heart.

When the Gibeonites appealed to Joshua, what did Joshua do and who did he take with him **(Joshua 10:7)**?

What did God say to Joshua as he moved forward with his army in **Joshua 10:8**?

There it is again. **"Joshua, do not be afraid."** No doubt, Joshua was a man of belief. He didn't just believe God, but he believed Him at His word. We will see Joshua's belief on the battlefield as he moves in God's power, trusts His Word, and manifests an audacious faith. A defining moment in Joshua's life, for sure.

Again, read through **Joshua 10:9-15**. What did Joshua pray for? What did God do? Ask God to stir your heart as you write your answer.

First, we need to address this amazing miracle. There have been many theories on what could have happened. To name a few… 1) God allowed light to remain in Gibeon, much like the Hebrews had light even when the Egyptians were in the dark **(Exodus 10:23)**; 2) The text is poetic and cannot be taken literally; 3) It was an eclipse that gave the appearance of a long day in which the sun did not set.

Now, write down exactly what the passage says **(Joshua 10:13)**.

With these words before you, are you inclined to believe the theories, or will you believe that it happened exactly the way the text says – that God stopped the sun from going down for "about a full day?" Did you know that on the ancient calendar, scientists say that there are 23 hours and 20 minutes unaccounted for? An interesting fact, don't you agree? *Surely the LORD was fighting for Israel (Joshua 10:14).*

Let's quickly cover what we discover about Joshua, the leader of Israel, in this passage.

Joshua exemplified the *soul* of a warrior!

In God's battle it's not about us fighting; it's about letting God fight for us. Joshua prayed! And then he moved forward in God's power. Perhaps he learned his lesson when he was deceived by the Gibeonites simply because he failed to pray. Now, when push comes to shove, Joshua shows what he's truly made of – a warrior spirit.

Until we let God fight for us, we will never experience the power of God or be used to move the hand of God. In fact, God fights so much better than we do. God is looking for mighty warriors to do His bidding and Joshua shows us exactly how it's done. LETTING GOD GO BEFORE US. When we let Him fight, we get to stand back and watch – watch Him come to our rescue, like He did for the Israelites by confusing their enemies and hurling large hailstones from heaven.

Let me ask you. Have you failed to pray about something? Are you fighting a battle in your own strength? If so, will you change your position? Will you become a warrior God can count on? Write down your thoughts.

Joshua exercised an *audacious* faith!

God honors a life of faith. The writer of Hebrews says, **"And without faith it is impossible to please God" (Hebrews 11:6)**. But according to James **"faith without works is useless" (James 2:20)**. In other words, true faith is accompanied by our deeds, our works. And in Joshua's case, he didn't just exercise faith, but he led with an *audacious* faith. The word audacious means, "Extremely bold or daring, recklessly brave, fearless." [3]

I'm not sure there is a prayer quite like the one Joshua prayed anywhere else in Scripture. It was… Bold! Daring! Brave! Fearless! What was he thinking? Asking God to keep the sun from going down? Really? I wonder if a few eyebrows were raised. What a warrior!

How are we instructed to pray, according to **1 John 5:14-15**?

As we conclude our lesson today, ponder this…

What man cannot do, God can!

Are you willing to pray the impossible? Are you willing to pray so big that reasoning cannot be figured into the equation? If you could muster up the same kind of boldness that Joshua exemplified on this day, then your faith will make headlines in the heavens. This is what great warriors are made of.

What is God asking you to do right now? What will you surrender so God can fight for you? How will you pray?

Day 4
Conquering the Land

I love stories about people who never gave up. They overcame great obstacles, faced huge giants, and survived strong opposition. In the end, they accomplished what they set out to do simply because they persevered and didn't buckle under pressure or back down when the going got tough. Inspiring quotes often move us. Here are a few that remind us not to give up:

God never said the journey would be easy, but He did say the arrival would be worthwhile. –Max Lucado

Perseverance must finish its work so that you may be mature and complete, not lacking anything. –James 1:4

Never, Never, Never give up. –Winston Churchill

Winners never quit and quitters never win. –Vince Lombardi

I have fought the good fight, I have finished the race, I have kept the faith. Now there is in store for me the crown of righteousness. –the Apostle Paul (2 Timothy 4:7-8)

By perseverance the snail reached the ark. –Charles Spurgeon

I am prepared to go anywhere, provided it be forward. I determined never to stop until I had come to the end and achieved my purpose. –David Livingstone

Are you inspired yet? Are you going to keep on keeping on? Joshua should serve as our example because he *never* gave up. He continues to move forward in God's power to conquer the land. Our lesson today will reveal one truly remarkable thing about Joshua that surely brought down God's favor: obedience. He did *everything* God told him to do, except the time he fell for the Gibeonites' deception. Perhaps he said, "Lesson learned! And I hope to never repeat it again."

We begin today where we left off yesterday. Joshua had prayed for daylight to catch his enemies and God answered his bold prayer by commanding the sun to stand still.

To set the stage, let's first recall what God said to Joshua at the beginning of his reign. What was it, according to **Joshua 1:7**?

Now read **Numbers 33:50-56**.

In one sentence, what did God command?

Why did say to drive out all the inhabitants?

Read **Joshua 10:16-43**. Comparing the previous word from God and this passage, would you say Joshua was a superb leader? Explain.

The first mention of the Canaanites is not in the book of Joshua. What do you find out in **Genesis 12:6**?

Yep! You're right! The Canaanites had occupied the land of Canaan for centuries, dating all the way back to Genesis. Do you think they knew about the God of Israel? What He demanded of His people? I would say *yes*. Word traveled! And of course, news of the miracles alone would have navigated back to the Canaanite people.

Sometimes people read the Old Testament and think of God as a tyrant because of all the bloodshed. But here's what people often overlook: not only is God loving, kind, compassionate, and merciful; He is also *just*. He *has* to punish sin because He is holy. And He commands holiness from His people.

In light of this, the Canaanites had heard about this holy God and they knew what He did to cities that continued in sin, e.g. Sodom and Gomorrah **(Genesis 29:14-25)**. But God is patient and gave them centuries to repent. Instead, they continued to bow to many different gods and involve themselves in horrible sinful practices, even sacrificing their own children.

Joshua reveals a truly outstanding quality of a superb leader: *obedience*.

How did such obedience pay off in the end for Joshua **(Joshua 24:31)**?

We will see throughout the book of Joshua that God honored obedience. And here's the thing: it hasn't changed. God still expects obedience from His people.

On the night before His betrayal, Jesus gave the great discourse on the vine and the branches **(John 15:1-8)**. In that same speech, He offered a word of exhortation. What was it **(John 15:10)**?

What is the benefit of obedience **(John 15:11)**?

Just like in the days of Joshua, there are beautiful rewards for obeying God. In addition to experiencing full joy – which is an awesome benefit – we become better leaders. One of the strongest mandates to becoming a great leader, like Joshua, is that we listen to Him and do everything He says.

Sadly, this has been lost in the church in a lot of ways. I've been in the church my whole life, and in ministry a good part of my adult life. I've seen great leaders and I've run across many not-so-good leaders. I've also been deeply hurt by church leaders. I've worked for Christians who were nasty to their clients, mean to their employees, and dishonest in their business transactions. Churches are full of these people. And many of them lead congregations. Perhaps this is why God is looking for exemplary leaders who will lead with integrity and obedience to His Word.

Will you answer the call to be that kind of leader? Write down your response.

Let's conclude our lesson today by observing a warning God gave. What did He say would happen if they did not completely drive out the inhabitants and destroy everything in the land **(Numbers 33:55-56)**?

God is always looking out for His people. He can see the future. He knows what will happen if we fail to listen. The land of Canaan was filled with every sort of evil and wicked behavior. False idols dominated daily worship. The apostle Paul said, **"Bad company corrupts good character" (1 Corinthians 15:33)**. You've seen it. I've seen it. Therefore, if His people – who were to bow to Him alone and live holy lives – let the people of Canaan continue to dwell in the land, they would become corrupted by their sinful practices. So to protect His people, everything had to be destroyed.

Joshua listened and obeyed. But as I said earlier, the land of Canaan was not completely conquered in Joshua's lifetime. God told Moses, **"Little by little I will drive them out before you, until you have increased enough to take possession of the land"** (Exodus 23:30). By the time we come to the book of Judges, the scene has changed. When conquering more of the land, they did *not* destroy the Canaanites **(Judges 1:21; 1:27-33)**.

What happened to Israel, according to **Judges 2:10-15**?

This was the beginning of their downfall. Throughout the whole Old Testament, Israel went through the following cycles.

Rebellion $\longrightarrow$ Defeat $\longrightarrow$ Repentance $\longrightarrow$ Restoration

After one whole cycle was complete, they would repeat it all over again. God *has* to judge sin. On two different occasions, they were driven from their land and became captive to the Babylonians and Assyrians. No doubt, it all began when they failed to listen to God and destroy everything in the land. The sin of their neighbors infiltrated into their daily life. God was faithful and He always restored them back to Him when they repented. But they could have been spared so much grief if they had only listened and obeyed in the first place.

Sin destroys everything. Sin reaps horrible consequences. The people of Israel can attribute to it.

Take a moment to fall before God and let Him examine your heart. Give Him every little crevice. Repent. And cry out to God to restore what's been broken because of sin.

Joshua serves as a wonderful role-model for all of us. He moved forward in obedience, even if it wasn't comfortable or popular. Therefore, God raised him as an esteemed leader and the people were blessed under his leadership. Remember this…

$$\text{Obedience} = \text{Success}$$

What is your take-away today? Write down your thoughts.

Day 5
Fighting Offensively

I've never fought in an earthly war. I've never had to endure the grueling months of boot camp, wearing thick fatigues in hot weather, aiming a gun at someone, being away from family for long stretches of time, or worried that I might never see my loved ones again. I thank God for those who have fought for the freedoms I enjoy in this country.

But I *do* know what it's like to look into the eyes of an angry enemy – a foe waiting to devour me. You do, too. The more faithful we are to God, the more Satan pursues us with a vengeance. This war is serious. Intense. Scary. In order to win, we need to march on down to the battlefield and fight back. We need to pursue the devil with a passion.

I said earlier in our study that we often don't know how to fight in this war. We've let Satan win far too much. Perhaps that's because we're not trained in all maneuvers. Hang in there with me today because I hope to expose a maneuver Joshua used in all battles: *offensive warfare*. Let's follow him into the land and experience how to fight offensively.

The book of Joshua can be divided into three main categories:
1) Entering the land (chapters 1-5)
2) Conquering the land (chapters 6-12)
3) Distribution of the land (chapters 13-24).

In our final week of study, we'll tackle the distribution of the land. Today concludes the conquering of the land.

First, ponder the definition of *offensive*: "an aggressive movement or attack." [4]

Read **Joshua 11:1-23**. Give a brief synopsis of this chapter.

Obviously, the kings in the north were in panic mode. Messengers brought word that the people of Israel were a mighty force not to be reckoned with. So they joined together to make one very strong coalition. Together, they planned and strategized how they would attack God's people. They would annihilate them one way or another.

But they were caught off guard by Joshua's army. What battle maneuver do you recognize in **Joshua 11:7**?

Oh, the element of surprise **(Joshua 11:7)**. Israel chased after their enemies and attacked them before they knew what hit them. In fact, this is one maneuver Joshua used in all the battles. They weren't about to sit back and wait to be attacked. Instead, they aggressively pursued them. Joshua was surely a mighty warrior.

It's been said that the Canaanites were powerful, fierce, and big. A mighty force. How does the Bible describe your enemy in **1 Peter 5:8**?

According to John **10:10**, what else is the devil called?

Satan is a master at taking what doesn't belong to him. He is a professional thief, preying on innocent victims. Victims unaware. He creeps in unnoticed and steals the land God has promised to us, just like the land of Canaan. He takes our joy, our peace, our security, our freedom, our confidence, and our hope. He also takes people we love, our families, our marriages, our homes, our ministries, and our jobs. Here's the thing: those things belong to us. All of them. They are gifts from God. They are *our* territory.

What has Satan stolen from you?

The devil has taken from me, I'll be honest. I don't know about you, but I want to be like Joshua and claim what is rightly mine. I will chase after my great enemy, pursuing him with everything inside me. There are two very crucial elements to winning a war – especially this spiritual war. We are to fight both *defensively* and *offensively*. I wish we had time to cover these tactics in depth, but we don't. So we will cover the basics and then you can do a more thorough study on your own.

Fighting defensively means that you enter the war fully protected. We are given a complete list of the pieces of armor we are to put on in **Ephesians 6:13-18.** List what they are and then do your own research on how to effectively wear them.

Today we will spend our time looking at how we can fight *offensively*. This was certainly a powerful ploy to Israel's victorious credit. Earlier in our study, we discussed *prayer* and the *Word of God*. These are the two most powerful weapons to use, for both defensive and offensive fighting. The devil flees every time we hurl the Sword of the Spirit – the Word of God – in his face. And he surely cringes when we bow our knees in prayer. But today, I hope to bring a few other offensive techniques before you. I'm not always adept at using these weapons, but I do plan to wield them a lot more.

Demolishing strongholds!

What truth do you find in **2 Corinthians 10:4-5**?

Satan's number one battleground is our minds. He slips in inconspicuously and speaks lies into our ears. *"You're not good enough. You're not loved. Your husband doesn't care. God isn't here. You can't get back up. You'll never get that friend back. You need that drink to help you. The world isn't bad. You need to accept their sin or lose them for good."*

Every word Satan breathes is against the knowledge of God **(2 Corinthians 10:5)**. The word *demolish* in this passage means, "to destroy." Therefore, we need to become skillful masters at discerning his lies and then destroying them by taking those thoughts captive – holding them in bondage so they won't hold us in bondage. And then saturate our minds with truth.

What lie are you believing right now? How do you know it's a lie? What will you do?

Binding and loosing!

What did Jesus say in **Matthew 16:19 (NIV)**?

These two weapons work together. We have the power to bind the forces of evil and loose the forces of good to work in their place. For example, we can bind the spirit of lying and loose the spirit of truth to work in its place.

Here are a few spirits we can bind and what we can loose in their place:

Bind the spirit of…	Loose the spirit of…
Unbelief	Belief
Division	Unity
Criticism	Praise
Doubt	Trust
Guilt	Honor
Condemnation	Approval

Is there a spirit you need to bind today? A spirit that has taken control in some area of your life? Write it down and then pray for the opposite spirit to be loosed. Perseverance is key when choosing to fight offensively.

The blood of Jesus and your testimony!

Write out **Revelation 12:11**.

When we bowed to Jesus' Lordship, He poured out His blood over us. His blood alone gives us the power to wage war offensively. The word testimony means "evidence or record." As you testify or "give evidence" to the power of God in your life, you wage spiritual offensive warfare. Jesus often told those He healed to go and tell others what He had done for them.

The Name of Jesus!

How are demons cast out, according to **Mark 16:17**?

I've heard stories of people literally stopping an attack because they spoke Jesus' Name. One phrase we should become adept at using is this: "In the Name of Jesus, I command you to flee." Satan cannot stand up against Jesus' Name and we – as His representatives – have the power to use His Name to fight offensively.

When we fight offensively, we go into Satan's territory and gain rather than lose. We gain back what's been awarded us. We cannot afford to sit comfortably in our homes, in our Christian groups, or in our churches. Not in the day in which we live. Joshua won each battle he fought by chasing down – and destroying – the enemy pursuing his people. We can, too.

Are you going to be a warrior like Joshua? Will you choose to fight for what's been stolen from you? Write out your thoughts.

1. LOGOS, *Be Strong*, Warren Wiersbe.
2. NIV Study Bible, p. 304.
3. http://www.dictionary.com/browse/audacious?s=t
4. http://www.dictionary.com/browse/offensive?s=t

Week 6
Settling the Land

Day 1
Never Too Old
Day 2
Painful Misunderstanding
Day 3
Farewell Address
Day 4
Covenant Renewal
Day 5
Finishing Strong

I love stories with strong finishes. My dad didn't grow up in a Christian home, but when his girls were young, he gave his heart to Jesus. Immediately his life changed and he threw himself into growing spiritually. And, thus, began a life of faith. He lived with integrity and godly character. And until the day he died, his faith never wavered. Many people can attribute to this. I would say that my dad finished strong.

The apostle Paul said to Timothy, **"I have fought the good fight, I have finished the race, I have kept the faith" (2 Timothy 4:7)**. In spite of years of overwhelming circumstances and horrible persecution, Paul's faith never wavered. He prayed, sought God with his whole heart, trained multitudes of believers in the Word of God, fought off cruel enemies, and walked his talk. To the Philippian believers, Paul wrote: **"For me, to live is Christ and to die is gain" (Philippians 1:21)**. Paul showed us how to live and how to die. He surely finished strong.

This week we come to the conclusion of Joshua – a bittersweet ending for me. We have watched God raise up a true warrior. He led with authority, power, and strength. His strategy and maneuvers worked to conquer the land. And the people of Israel were blessed to serve under his leadership. The race is almost over for Joshua. The finish line in sight. He must be tired, worn out from years of battling his enemies. But he won't stop until God tells him it's over. No wonder he's considered one of heaven's mightiest warriors.

Let's follow Joshua into the Promised Land as he divides it up between the twelve tribes of Israel. Our lesson this week will cover portions of the remainder of the book of Joshua. Stay engaged as I'm sure God isn't done pouring His Word into your heart through Joshua.

Day 1
Never Too Old

Joshua was not only a powerful warrior and a great leader, but this week, we discover another position he held: *administrator*. And I must say that he handled this position impeccably. Our study today covers **Joshua 13-19**. I know it seems like a lot of ground to cover, but we will just skim over a good portion of it.

For reference sake, the twelve sons of Jacob (the twelve tribes) are: Rueben, Simeon, Levi, Judah, Dan, Naphtali, Gad, Asher, Issachar, Zebulun, Joseph and Benjamin. Joseph's inheritance went to his two sons: Manasseh and Ephraim **(Genesis 48:5)**. If you're visual and love geography, here's a map of Israel and the distribution of the land to the twelve tribes.

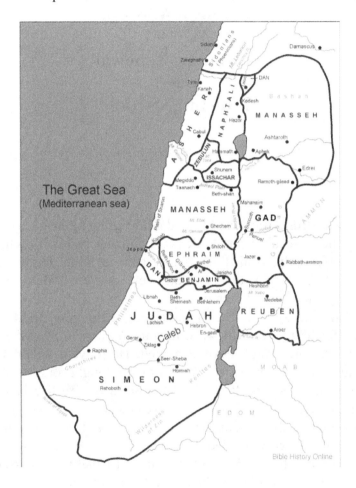

You may want to glance through **chapters 13-19** to get a feel of how the land was distributed among the twelve tribes.

Not all the tribes received an inheritance of land. What tribe was ruled out and why, according to **Joshua 13:14**?

Look back at **Deuteronomy 10:8-9** and **18:1-8**. What further information do these passages reveal about the Levites?

Instead of portions of land, what were the Levites granted **(Joshua 14:3-4)**?

It was a true privilege to be of the tribe of Levi. Their daily life was centered on God. Certainly my life's passion! They served in the tabernacle, and later the temple. They were teachers of the Law. And they received portions of the offerings and sacrifices the people were commanded to bring to God. Life for the Israelites focused on religious practices, and the Levites were set apart from the general population to serve God and to serve the people.

God chose *not* to give land to them perhaps for a couple reasons: 1) He didn't want the responsibilities of land ownership to distract them from their spiritual responsibilities; and 2) They were scattered among the people to be "salt and light" as they taught the Law. The Levites were to pour truth into the lay people and remind them of God's commands. So rather than receiving a portion of God's real estate, the Levites got the Lord of the land.

It seems that the Levitical priesthood has been passed to New Testament believers. Who are we, and what are our responsibilities, based on the following references?

1 Peter 2:5:

1 Corinthians 10:31:

Matthew 5:13-16:

The Levitical priesthood was not to be exalted to an elevated position, but to be wholly and completely surrendered to God. The same is true for us. Review the previous passages and write down what it means to you to be a royal priesthood, a holy nation.

Let's conclude today's lesson with an interesting scenario. Right in the middle of Joshua's administrative duties – dividing out the land – he receives a visitor with a request. Slowly read **Joshua 14:6-15** and summarize briefly.

What are your first thoughts about this scene?

This scenario makes me smile. I wonder if Joshua smiled, too. I want to yell, "Go, Caleb." Even in that day, eighty-five was old. But dear ole' elderly Caleb didn't let his age stop him. He was still running hard and ready to fight the enemy to take what belonged to him. What I love about his request is that he didn't ask for an easy city. No! He asked for the hill country (granted it was given to him already), where giants (Anakites were men of large stature) lived and their cities were large and fortified. No doubt, these were a people that wouldn't go down easy. But Caleb's faith was still as strong as it was on the day he came back with a good report of the land **(Numbers 13:30)**. He knew that God would fight for him.

Elderly people today often think that when they get to a certain age, they've done their work and now it's time for the younger ones to step up. Maybe society and the church make them feel this way. So they take a back seat, sit in their recliner, and retire from God's work. Well, this is wrong on so many levels. The younger generation needs to be mentored. They need to be led by those who have walked the faith. Seasoned believers have so much wisdom and life experience to pass on. Instead, they are often pushed in a corner and forgotten.

Caleb is such a role-model for us.

What does **Galatians 6:9-10** say?

God wants to use us no matter how old we are. The last two years of his life, Paul spent in Rome under house arrest. He was free to pursue his calling, but not free to travel. We are told that during this time, Paul **"welcomed all who came to him. Boldly and without hindrance he preached the kingdom of God and taught about the Lord Jesus Christ" (Acts 28:30-31)**. While the circumstances were not favorable and he was probably 60-62 years of age, he used *every* opportunity presented to him.

Billy Graham preached well into his 80's. Back in the day, he was young and robust, with a powerful voice. As he aged, his hands shook a little, his walk was a tad unsteady, and his voice quivered. But he still moved forward in the call on his life and preached the gospel to the masses. Like Caleb, he was just as strong in his old age as he was when he was young.

Have you prayed for opportunities? Are you paying attention to the opportunities before you? What are they? And how will you use them?

In the midst of where you are in life, what do the following verses mean to you?

Philippians 1:6:

2 Chronicles 15:7:

Do these verses give you a firmer purpose to keep going? How?

In conclusion, take a moment to write out what inspired you about both the Levitical priesthood and Caleb:

Levitical priesthood:

Caleb:

Day 2
Painful Misunderstanding

If we could sum up Joshua, we might say that he was a jack of all trades. He could do just about anything, and he did it well. Joshua was a military strategist, a superb leader, a man of exemplary faith, and a detailed administrator. What a guy! He was surely a winner in heaven's corner. And I hope he's a winner in your book, too. I can't wait to meet him one day.

Begin by skimming over the following chapters. What is the basic theme in each one?

Joshua 20:

Joshua 21:

The cities of refuge were set up as a safe-guard for the people. If they accidentally killed someone, they could run to one of these cities and receive a fair trial. If they were found innocent, then they could live there and be protected from those seeking to kill them. God is always looking out for His people.

Now for the remainder of our lesson, I want to focus on **Joshua 22**. Read this chapter and give a brief synopsis.

To understand what's happening in this chapter, we need to visit a conversation that the tribes of Reuben and Gad had with Moses in **Numbers 32:1-33**. You may want to read it before continuing. The land of Israel – the land promised to God's people – included land on both the east side and the west side of the Jordan River. But the Israelites would settle on the *west* side of the river. The river would serve as a barrier between them and their enemies. But the tribes of Reuben, Gad and the half-tribe of Manasseh wanted to settle on the east side of the river for the rich pastureland. So they asked Moses if they could build their homes east of the river. Moses complied, but under one condition. The fighting men would stay on the west side of the river and help the other tribes out until they were settled. The leaders agreed.

While it seemed like a good idea to settle on the east side of the river, scholars believe it wasn't such a wise decision. Here are a few reasons why:

1. The decision was based on material gain, not on spiritual values.
2. The decision divided the nation.
3. The decision separated them from the blessings of Canaan.
4. The decision would make them further from the tabernacle.
5. The decision would make them closer to their enemies.

With this information before us, we now come to **Joshua 22**. Explain what's going on in **verses 1-9**.

Can you picture the scene? It took about seven years to conquer the land. So for seven years these men were separated from their families while they fought against powerful enemies for their brothers' land. Now the war is over and the men are returning home. And not empty handed either. Because of their loyalty to Moses, Joshua, and their Israelite brothers, they were given great wealth, large herds of livestock, silver, gold, bronze, iron, and a great quantity of clothing. Amazing, huh? Something tells me that while their bodies were tired, and some perhaps suffered from physical pain, their spirits soared. As these men of valor lugged their spoils from war (to share with their brothers and sisters left at home), hope was rekindled. Finally they could plan their future.

What does **John 15:9-11** tell you about obedience?

I see a formula at work in this passage. Here it is…

Obedience = Remaining in His love = Joy

God has always been in the habit of blessing obedience. We would fare so much better and have greater joy in our lives if we would just obey His commands, instead of trying to do it our way.

Is there something you're trying to do your own way? What does God's Word say? How will you change it?

Now, let's continue with our story.

What happened next **(Joshua 22:10)**?

The purpose of the altar was simply a reminder to the other ten tribes of Israel, and to their neighbors, that they belonged to Israel. Maybe they were beginning to feel isolated and separated from their countrymen. Either way, they innocently built an altar.

How did the Israelites learn about the altar **(Joshua 22:11)**?

Continue with **Joshua 22:12-20**.

What did their Israelite brothers believe?

What did they do with their assumptions?

Have you ever been misunderstood? Explain what happened.

What started out as a joyous occasion and an innocent gesture almost caused another war. Why? Because the Israelites jumped to conclusions. They were acting on hearsay. Someone squealed: *Guess what those three rebellious tribes have done? They built an altar, when clearly God told us that we are to worship Him in one place and have only one altar.* This report stirred their hearts to anger. So they sent representatives to throw the Law into their faces.

What words of wisdom are found in **Proverbs 18:13**?

Acting on hearsay destroys relationships, creates conflict, causes irreparable damage, and can ruin a good reputation. Nothing good ever comes from gossip. Asking questions first and checking the source(s) is always better than spreading unwarranted babble. I see this all the time on the Internet. Recently a Facebook friend shared an article about why a notable minister of the gospel was a heretic. I felt a flame in my spirit getting hotter and hotter as I began to read one man's harsh words about someone I truly respected. And then I began to read the comments. People believed it. Everything inside me said that it wasn't true and I couldn't find any other evidence to support these claims. But these false accusations had already been spread worldwide.

The damage could have been catastrophic. Before believing something, we should *always* check the facts.

Initially, the Israelites wanted to bring war on those "rebellious" nations. Instead, and to everyone's benefit, they sent representatives to get the facts. Hence, the scenario ended on a positive note.

Read **Joshua 22:21-34** and write down the end of the story.

Conclude with your thoughts on today's lesson. What did God speak to you about?

Day 3
Farewell Address

There are hundreds of Bible studies on the market today. But what I've found is that most of them are topical. I'm not saying there's anything wrong with topical studies, but there's something amazing about going through a book of the Bible. It helps us to understand the chronology of the Bible and it gives us the opportunity to study it the way God gave it to us – in books. I'm drawn to churches that teach through whole books of the Bible. When I was growing up, it took my pastor five years to teach through Romans. Five years! Still makes me smile.

The book of Joshua spans some twenty-five years. As we come to the conclusion of the book – and as the people settle into their new land – Joshua calls together the **"elders, leaders, judges and officials" (Joshua 23:2)** for some final thoughts. He knows his time on earth is nearing the end and his mind is swirling with things he needs to say before he dies. Important matters he hopes they will grasp and embrace. He looks out over this crowd and sees strong men full of life and vitality. Something tells me that he's a little teary-eyed remembering everything they've gone through together. Then he speaks.

How does he begin his message **(Joshua 23:2)**?

By human standards, he was very old. The Bible tells us that Joshua died at the ripe old age of 110 **(Joshua 24:29)**. And the message he has for the people on this day was probably spoken shortly before he died. I wonder if he was reminded of the day *he* stood in the crowd while his predecessor, Moses, spoke to the people shortly before he died. He hopes that the people before him can see the same fire in his eyes as he saw in Moses' eyes. He hopes they will make a commitment in their hearts, as he had done way back then, to follow God and walk in His ways. So he silently prays. Leaning on his staff, and with a quivery voice, he begins.

Joshua's message **(Joshua 23:3-16)** can be divided into three sections – *Inspiration, Instruction,* and *Warning*. When these three things are intermixed, motivation is a beautiful outcome.

Let's chew on each of these sections today.

Inspiration!

Compile the main themes in **Joshua 23:3-5**.

Inspiration is when something we see, hear, or experience awakens our senses and often motivates us to pursue deeper passions. When the inspiration comes from a God-story, our faith can climb to new levels, our appetite for God can increase, and such testimonies can serve as a catalyst to transform our kingdom work. The other night I watched an inspiring movie about a man who gave up a million-dollar career to save orphans from living on the streets. Absolutely remarkable! This true story revived my spirit. Inspiration is something we all need in the humdrum daily grind of life. Otherwise, we can get complacent.

The people are in their new land and settled in their homes. The war is over and the great miracles behind them. Joshua knows that soon life can become ordinary and routine. And he's also aware that the influences of their ungodly neighbors can easily creep in unnoticed. So he begins by helping them to remember.

What were they to remember **(Joshua 23:3)**?

Think back and write out some things God did for them.

It's easy to forget. As time moves forward and life happens, we can quickly forget all that God has done for us. It's then that our excitement for God takes a back seat to earthly things. And without passion, our light slowly goes out. I'm pretty sure that right now you and I need inspiration. Let me encourage you to recall what God has done for you. In the space provided, write down a couple God-amazements in your life, either personal experiences or Scriptural truths.

Sometimes inspiration can be in the form of God-promises. What promise did Joshua remind the people of in **Joshua 23:4-5**?

As your heart is beginning to stir, what promise is God reminding you of? What will you do with this promise?

Instruction!

Observe **Joshua 23:6-10**. List each piece to this "instruction" puzzle.

I know plenty of believers who choose to walk their own way and live the way they see fit. But here's how I look at it. Since Jesus came to this earth and died to redeem me, and He has offered me abundant life here and eternal life in heaven – including many awesome benefits – why wouldn't I live my life for Him? Why wouldn't I obey His commands? Why wouldn't I surrender my will, my desires, and my plans to Him? Out of extreme gratitude, obedience should be a natural response. Also, obedience to God keeps the enemy at bay. Perhaps that's what Joshua was trying to tell the people.

Fill in the blanks from the following verses:

Verse 7: Do not _____ **the names of their gods or swear by them.**

Verse 8: You are to _____ _____ **to the LORD your God.**

Verse 11: Be careful to _____ **the LORD your God.**

We live thousands of years later, but we still struggle with some of the same things: namely idols. We need Joshua's instruction as much as the people standing before him did. Our idols aren't statues, but we bow to money, fame, people, career, education, entertainment, status, and talents and gifts. Putting anything above God – or in the place of God – is idolatry. So Joshua clearly sets down the standard for God's holy people: don't bow to idols, but hold fast to the LORD your God and love Him. The phrase *hold fast* means to "cling to, or cleave." [1]

Do an evaluation right now. Is there an idol you are bowing to? What is it?

How will you hold fast to the LORD your God? How will you love Him above all else? Write down your thoughts.

Warning!

In a couple sentences, what is the warning in **Joshua 23:12-16**?

We're not sure how long the people of God heeded this warning, but we do learn that their future was wracked by war, death, destruction, isolation, and captivity. Why? Simply because they failed to listen and obey. Joshua would have been shaking his head after a lifetime of obedience to God. We would do well to listen to God's warning, too.

How will you respond to Joshua's message today? Will you need to make any changes?

Here's one last thought: this message was spoken to the leaders and the elders. Therefore, it was intended to be passed down from the top. So let's remember to ALWAYS inspire, encourage, and teach truth as we lead in our circles of influence.

Day 4
Covenant Renewal

As a leader my responsibility is *not* to bring people to hear the message, make people engaged in studying God's Word, convict people of their sin, or cause people to live faithfully. Those things are the Holy Spirit's responsibility. My responsibility as a leader is surely to encourage these things, to teach them, and to try my best to live them. My responsibility is to hold up the Word of God and to lead in truth. My responsibility is to shine a spotlight onto the ways God says we are to live. I pray I will be the kind of the leader who lives what she speaks. Not perfectly, but humbly.

Joshua was surely the kind of leader that brought honor to his God. He moved forward with a spear in his hand and promises tucked in his heart. He would be the first to tell us that it wasn't an easy journey, but a necessary one. And surely a profitable work that ended in a glorious outcome. What we see in Joshua is not the greatness of this leader, but the greatness of his God. His faith is contagious and his warrior skills unsurpassed.

Today we continue with Joshua's final message. He's determined not to die before he speaks the words burning in his heart. As you picture yourself standing in the crowd and hanging onto every word that comes from Joshua's mouth, keep in mind that our purpose is to build a bridge from Old Testament practices to New Testament living. We will see how the words Joshua said before the people on this day will directly relate to 21st century believers.

Read **Joshua 24** (out loud if you can).

This chapter is filled with Scriptural treasures. Joshua begins by observing four things God did for Israel, and then concludes with a strong exhortation. A perfect way to end a mighty warrior's legacy.

Four things God did for Israel...

1) God *chose* Israel (24:1-4)!

How does Joshua describe the choosing in **Joshua 24:1-4**?

Explain the choosing further in **Deuteronomy 7:7-8**.

When were you chosen by God, according to **Ephesians 1:4**?

We often think that *we* chose God, but the opposite is actually true. God chose us at the beginning of the world, and by grace alone. He ran hard after you and vowed to not let you slip out of His hands. When you said *yes* to Him, He accepted you and offered you every spiritual blessing **(Ephesians 1:3)**. What an honor to be chosen by the God of the universe!

2) God *delivered* Israel (24:5-7)!

How did God deliver Israel based on **Joshua 24:5-7**?

Relate our deliverance in **Galatians 5:1** to Israel.

No one wants to live as a slave. The Israelites were subjected to harsh conditions by slave masters that didn't care about them. They imposed their ungodly rules and guidelines to a people set apart for holy purposes. Sin enslaves us. When sin reins in our life, it's like we've been taken captive – forced to do what we don't want to do. But Jesus came for this very reason. Jesus' blood delivered us from the sting of sin and death and offered us freedom. How blessed we are.

3) God *guided* and *protected* Israel (24:8-10)!

How did God guide and protect the Israelites in the wilderness **(Joshua 24:8-10)**?

Look up **John 16:13**. Who guides us? How does He guide us?

What does Jesus pray in **John 17:15**?

Like Israel, we are never alone and God never expects us to walk this journey without help. Sometimes the pathway is treacherous, with plenty of hills and curves. We ask: Am I on the road God wants me on? Am I living the way I should be living? But don't forget that we have an enemy who is hiding – just waiting for the perfect opportunity to snare us into his trap. He's very deceptive as he entangles God's people. But we can be assured that the Holy Spirit guides us into truth and Jesus protects us. So, we're good!

4) God *gave* Israel their land (24:11-13)!

What does Joshua tell the people of gaining the land promised **(Joshua 24:11-13)**?

Ponder **Hebrews 9:15**. What has God promised us?

God moved His people for generations toward the inheritance He would give them – a new land. And He delivered on His promise. The entering into the Promised Land is a look into what's in the future for you and me. We can be assured that He will give us our inheritance because He is a God who keeps His promises. There's no earthly inheritance we could ever claim that is better than the one God has waiting for us. I'm excited. Are you?

Look back over the four things that bridge the gap between the Old Testament and the New Testament. Pick at least one and write down how you've experienced it in your life or the hope it gives you.

Joshua is not finished with his message. A strong godly leader is one who speaks truth and leads by example. But here's another impactful component: he also challenges and exhorts his followers to action. There are a few pastors and speakers I love to listen to because they always seem to propel me into action. I wonder if the people listening to Joshua responded in a similar way. Joshua was old but spoke with great authority. God was the one speaking through him on this day. Perhaps some fell to their knees while others clapped and cheered on their revered leader. No matter, this message has been stored in heaven's archives under the title of *noble* speeches.

Let's conclude our lesson today with a "call to action" challenge.

- **Decide who you will serve (24:14-24)!**

Read through **Joshua 24:14-24** and summarize the challenge Joshua brought.

The land was still filled with ungodly people – people who served and worshiped false deities. But the nation of Israel was set apart for holiness and their God was a jealous God. He made it clear from the early days in the wilderness that undivided allegiance would not be tolerated. So they must decide – will they worship and serve the surrounding false gods, or will they devote themselves completely to the God who called them as His own, delivered them from slavery, and brought them into a new land?

How did the people respond **(Joshua 24:21** and **24)**?

What did Joshua do in the presence of all the people in **Joshua 24:25-27**?

Let me ask you: Who is your allegiance to? Are you fully devoted to God or are you divided? Right now is a perfect time to decide. Write out your prayer.

Day 5
Finishing Strong

You've probably read the popular poem written by Linda Ellis called, *The Dash*:

*"I read of a man who stood to speak at the funeral of a friend.
He referred to the dates on the tombstone
from the beginning...to the end. He noted that
first came the date of birth and spoke
the following dates with tears, but he said what mattered
most of all was the dash between those years..."* [2]

The poem goes on to say that what will really matter at the end of your life is how you lived your dash. What will people remember about you? Will they talk about how you loved others? Will they testify about how you walked your talk? Did you invest in helping your brothers and sisters mature in Christ? Was your love for Jesus authentic? Were lives changed because of how you lived? Hence, we should live our lives as though today might be the last. We should spend the majority of our time accumulating eternal things because that's how we will finish strong.

We can genuinely say that Joshua finished strong. And now his time on the earth is wrapping up. He calls the nation before him and leaves his people with some final thoughts and challenges as they settle in the land God gave to them. A bittersweet moment for him, I'm sure.

But something tells me that Joshua is proud of the way he lived. He led with a fierce resolve. He followed God wholeheartedly and never drifted from the Book of the Law. He made Moses' legacy proud. And he trained a nation how to be mighty warriors.

Joshua speaks his last message and then sends the people back to their homes **(Joshua 24:28)**.

We conclude our Bible study today with the final words in the book of Joshua.

Read **Joshua 24:29-33** and summarize briefly.

What pieces of information do you learn about Joshua **(Joshua 24:29-30)**?

Compare **Joshua 19:49-50** with the previous verses. What did he do in the remaining years of his life?

Leading God's people faithfully into the land promised has perks. One of the perks is that Joshua got the pick of the land to settle in. And he picked the hill country of Ephraim, a wooded piece of land with fertile and lush valleys. He spent his final years building up the cities in that area. Joshua's vision was as strong and sharp as it was in the beginning. He was not going to spend his final days fishing and laying in a hammock. The war was over but the cities needed to be built. Now we can add *builder* to Joshua's impressive resumé.

What work is God calling you to? You may want to pray about it and then write down what God tells you. How will you respond? What will you do to follow His leading?

Write out **Joshua 24:31**.

Joshua's life was just summed up in one verse. He served God well and he led forth in truth. He never wavered from the faith. What a heritage to pass to the next generation. No wonder Joshua is considered heaven's mightiest warrior. This is called finishing strong.

Let's go back to what God said to Joshua at the beginning of his reign **(Joshua 1:6-9)**. How do you know that Joshua lived these words?

We may live in a modern world but the Word of God should never be modernized. The Bible warns us that we should never add to or take away from God's Word **(Revelation 22:18-19)**. It's complete. Leaders often pick and choose what they want to teach, and sometimes they leave important topics out because they're afraid of offending people.

The apostle Paul said to the church at Galatia: **"I am astonished that you are so quickly deserting the one who called you by the grace of Christ and are turning to a different gospel – which is really no gospel at all" (Galatians 1:6-7)**. You see, the leaders in this church were teaching the New Testament Christians that they needed to be circumcised like the Old Testament saints. But Jesus abolished that practice at the cross. Paul exposed this warped theology with a warning.

The church, the family, and every aspect of our lives would fare so much better if everything found its basis on the great instruction **(Joshua 1:6-9)** God gave to Joshua.

So here's my concluding exhortation:

Live your life with these words from **Joshua 1:6-9** before you in everything you do. Then you will be successful in God's eyes and you'll finish strong, whenever that time comes.

How will you do it?

Review your study on Joshua. What principles are burning in your heart right now? What did God reveal to you? How does He want you to live?

Thank you taking this journey with me. Something tells me that God has already begun to raise you up to be a mighty warrior, just like Joshua.

---

1. *Zondervan NIV Exhaustive Concordance* (Grand Rapids, MI: Zondervan Publishing Co.), 1387.
2. http://www.linda-ellis.com/read-the-dash--by-linda-ellis.html

About the Author

    There is nothing that gives me greater joy than to watch God open up people's hearts to the truth of His Word. Words cannot describe the joy in my heart every time I hear what God is doing in the lives of His people through one of my Bible studies. Sometimes I think I can hear heaven's hosts shouting "Halleluiah."

    It has been a true privilege writing this Bible study on Joshua. I started with a blank canvas and ended with a treasure. There is such valuable insight within the pages of this study. Joshua has shown me how to be a great leader, a mighty warrior, and a true servant of the Most High God. I hope his story will reach many within the Church and that God will raise up multitudes of warriors to do His bidding. The war is escalating and I believe that I'm now more prepared to walk to the battlefield and fight this battle raging in the heavenly realms. I trust that you will gain incredible truth as you study Joshua.

In Him,

Sheryl

Sheryl Pellatiro is an active Bible study teacher, author, and speaker. You can find more Bible studies and encouraging blog posts on her website – www.solidtruthministries.com and on her blog – www.sherylpellatiro.com.

Other Bible Studies

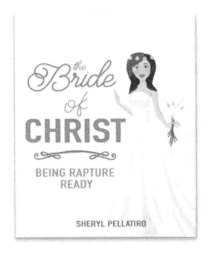  

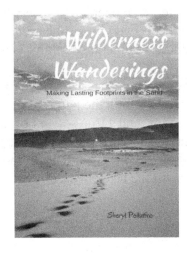 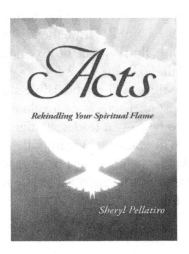

Visit our website for more resources, to sign up for our weekly blog, and/or to receive all the latest up-to-date happenings with the ministry:

www.solidtruthministries.com

We are a ministry committed to equipping believers in the Word of God through Bible study materials, Bible study classes (both locally and nationally), online Bible classes, leadership workshops, conferences, blogs, and many other venues.

Our Mission...

To build up God's people on a firm foundation.

Our Focus...

To come along side you, pray for you, and encourage you through the many biblical resources God has given to us that will help you draw closer to Him. This ministry is designed to energize your current relationship and walk with our Lord, or perhaps assist you in beginning a new walk with Him. We are here for you.

Our Vision...

To strengthen and empower believers globally with solid truth, and equip them with life skills for their family and community. It's also our vision to bring the truth of God's Word to those who may be questioning what they believe.

Please help us take the message of God's Word into your community.

Made in the USA
Monee, IL
24 September 2024